Praise for *Self-Portrait with Dogwood*

"An arboreal memoir, an autobiographical dendrology: Merrill, like the dogwood seeds and seedlings, roams the planet, appearing or pausing at unexpected moments in history. The migrant trees sink their roots in various foreign soils; the man, though wandering—even in zones of war—remains rooted in the humus of poetry."

— ELIOT WEINBERGER

"Christopher Merrill is a national treasure, both as a writer and a global warrior for literature and witness. In a fine career of making exquisite books, *Self-Portrait with Dogwood* might be his most moving. Beauty rises from every page. Going on my short list of favorite books—I will refer to it and teach it for the rest of my life, like I do with Bashō and Hanshan. A quiet classic."

— LUIS ALBERTO URREA

"How wise of the U.S. State Department to send Christopher Merrill around the globe as a poet-ambassador. I can't imagine anyone better equipped to represent us to a suffering and turbulent world. His attentive ear and eye, his keen mind, his compassionate heart, his courage and eloquence are all richly displayed in this engrossing book. The stories he tells here—about woods and waters, poetry and soccer, about literary heroes, an ailing daughter, and a dying friend—are suffused by Merrill's devotion to merc[...] [...]nd[...] with the ineffable power w[...]

"Christopher Merrill speaks to the essential and too often buried part of us that intuits the relatedness of all things (human beings and nature, love and war, shame and desire) and investigates the way those intersections urge some of us toward metaphor, toward a life dedicated to the making of art. *Self-Portrait with Dogwood* makes a case for a new type of memoir in which the self—rather than being spotlighted—is but one slender thread in an intricate weave that reaches across species, centuries, and time zones. This is an elegant, intelligent, deeply compelling, and necessary book."

— PAM HOUSTON,
author of *Contents May Have Shifted*

"How do we attach meaning to human existence? Merrill's memoir turns to the dogwood tree as talisman, a presence from his childhood through a life richly textured with natural, literary, and cultural history. His artful reflections on friendship, family, poetry, transplanting trees, and global diplomacy show how 'giving voice to nonhuman perspectives' may indeed be essential to cultivating our humanity."

— ALISON HAWTHORNE DEMING,
author of *Zoologies: On Animals and the Human Spirit*

Self-Portrait with Dogwood

Also by Christopher Merrill

POETRY

Workbook

Fevers & Tides

Watch Fire

Brilliant Water

7 Poets, 4 Days, 1 Book, with Marvin Bell, István László Geher, Ksenia Golubovich, Simone Inguanez, Tomaž Šalamun, and Dean Young

Necessities

Boat

After the Fact: Scripts & Postscripts, with Marvin Bell

ESSAYS

The Forest of Speaking Trees: An Essay on Poetry

Your Final Pleasure: An Essay on Reading

NONFICTION

The Old Bridge: The Third Balkan War and the Age of the Refugee

The Grass of Another Country: A Journey Through the World of Soccer

Only the Nails Remain: Scenes from the Balkan Wars

Things of the Hidden God: Journey to the Holy Mountain

The Tree of the Doves: Ceremony, Expedition, War

EDITED WORKS

Outcroppings: Selected Writings of John McPhee

The Forgotten Language: Contemporary Poets and Nature

From the Faraway Nearby: Georgia O'Keeffe as Icon, with
  Ellen Bradbury

What Will Suffice: Contemporary American Poets on the Art of Poetry,
  with Christopher Buckley

The Four Questions of Melancholy: New & Selected Poems, by
  Tomaž Šalamun

The Way to the Salt Marsh: A John Hay Reader

The New Symposium: Poets and Writers on What We Hold in Common,
  with Nataša Ďurovičová

Flash Fiction International: Very Short Stories from Around the World,
  with Robert Shapard and James Thomas

TRANSLATIONS

Anxious Moments, prose poems by Aleš Debeljak, with the author

The City and the Child, poems by Aleš Debeljak, with the author

Even Birds Leave the World: Selected Poems of Ji-woo Hwang, with
  Won-Chung Kim

Because of the Rain: A Selection of Korean Zen Poems, with
  Won-Chung Kim

Scale and Stairs: Selected Poems of Heeduk Ra, with Won-Chung Kim

Translucency: Selected Poems of Chankyung Sung, with
  Won-Chung Kim

The Growth of a Shadow: Selected Poems of Taejoon Moon, with
  Won-Chung Kim

The Night of the Cat's Return, poems by Chanho Song, with
  Won-Chung Kim

Christopher Merrill

Self-Portrait with Dogwood

Trinity University Press | SAN ANTONIO

for Tom Gavin

Published by Trinity University Press
San Antonio, Texas 78212

Cover design by ALSO
Book design by BookMatters

ISBN 978-1-59534-809-8 paperback
ISBN 978-1-59534-810-4 ebook

Trinity University Press strives to produce its books using
methods and materials in an environmentally sensitive manner.
We favor working with manufacturers that practice sustainable
management of all natural resources, produce paper using
recycled stock, and manage forests with the best possible
practices for people, biodiversity, and sustainability. The press
is a member of the Green Press Initiative, a nonprofit program
dedicated to supporting publishers in their efforts to reduce
their impacts on endangered forests, climate change, and forest-
dependent communities.

The paper used in this publication meets the minimum
requirements of the American National Standard for
Information Sciences—Permanence of Paper for Printed Library
Materials, ANSI 39.48-1992.

CIP data on file at the Library of Congress

21 20 19 18 17 | 5 4 3 2 1

Contents

I never saw a tree that was one tree in particular.

—ANNIE DILLARD, *Pilgrim at Tinker Creek*

Prologue

The average lifespan of a flowering dogwood is eighty years, and at the approach of my sixtieth birthday it occurred to me that I might create a self-portrait in relation to a tree that from an early age I have regarded as a talisman. Not a memoir, strictly speaking, but a literary exploration of certain events through the lens of nature—a taking stock of a journey destined to end in the earth. In the course of researching dogwoods, the common name for the woody plants of the *Cornus* genus found in temperate climates throughout North America, Europe, and Asia, I realized that a number of formative moments in my life had some connection to the tree named, according to one writer, because its fruit was not fit for a dog. In the nursery trade, dogwoods are called ornamentals, their flowering a highpoint of spring. But they serve critical functions in the ecosystem as well, and since they have informed so much of my life it seemed to me that an extended meditation on the intersection between personal and natural history might hold interest, if for no other reason than to offer a different way of thinking about the tradition of writing memoirs.

A small deciduous tree, the flowering dogwood belongs to the understory in a hardwood forest, occupying the middle space between the ground and sky, providing nectar for pollinating insects, branches and foliage and fruit for perching and nesting songbirds, nutrients for the soil, ingredients for medicines, wood for bowls and shuttles and tools, and an open invitation for an aging man to reflect on his walk in the sun, to reconsider his relationship to nature, to pay attention to the worlds revolving in his memory, his imagination, and all around him.

Dismal Harmony

I built a fort under the dogwood tree, at the edge of the woods separating our property from the road to the Wrights' house. Mr. Wright was a Native American (Mohawk, if memory serves, not Lenni-Lenape, the original inhabitants of northern New Jersey), which barely figured into my calculations when I played war with his son Michael, our childhood being framed by the Cuban missile crisis and and the Vietnam War. Our battles were waged between Russians and Americans, not cowboys and Indians; from the base of the dogwood, in a trench dug with sticks and stocked with Fritos, I took aim at my friend, who was hiding in the brambles, aiming at me.

Both Michael and his older brother, John, spoke with lisps, which I held against them. I never liked John, who was not athletic, and when I was cruel to Michael, who was a little weaker than I, they would run and tell their father. He was a lean, dark man with heavily lined features and veins popping out of his arms; his sons attributed this to hard work. Indeed he was always in his yard, cutting the grass, raking leaves, keeping an eye on us. I feared his gaze, even as I hoped that one day veins would pop out of my arms too.

In the meantime I roamed around our village, a patchwork of forests, dairy farms, and houses, some dating to the colonial era, crisscrossed by streams flowing from the surrounding hills. I explored the shuttered iron and mica mines and the remains of forges, kilns, gristmills; fished for suckers in the brook by the baseball field; unearthed arrowheads in the tracks where the Rock-A-Bye-Baby Railroad used to run. Down the road from my grandparents' place, in Jockey Hollow, was the Wick House, which had a story. A zigzagging split-rail fence bound the field north of the house, where a hundred soldiers from the Continental Army lay buried, victims of disease and the harshest winters of the Revolutionary War. The most consequential insurrection on the road to independence took shape here, which in turn gave Captain Henry Wick's youngest daughter, Tempe (short for Temperance), an occasion to become a war heroine.

Captain Wick had acquired 1,400 acres of timber and pasture by the time of his death, on the winter solstice in 1780; some of it was used to house a resentful brigade of the Pennsylvania Line under the command of General "Mad" Anthony Wayne. This was a difficult time for General Wayne's troops, who were for the most part landless immigrants from Ireland. They lived twelve to a hut, they had not been paid for months, and after three years of fighting their twenty-dollar enlistment bounties seemed paltry compared to the thousand-dollar bonuses that other states were offering new recruits. Shortages of food and clothing left many starving and barefoot in the snow. General Wayne, a charismatic leader described by historian Theodore Thayer as "a superb fighter if not a brilliant strategist," could not quell their rising anger. Those who did not desert grew more desperate with every blizzard that December. Some decided to march to Philadelphia to demand their back pay, and in the days before the revolt they foraged through the countryside for food and horses.

Things came to a head on New Year's night. What sparked the mutiny was the arrival of government agents dispensing cash to soldiers who had served for just six months, ignoring the pleas of those who refused to accept Philadelphia's claim that they had signed up for the duration of the war. Hard drinking exacerbated their feelings, and when a rocket was fired to muster the troops to the parade ground all hell broke loose. The mutineers set upon the officers who ordered them to return to their quarters, wounding several and killing one, who had pointed his half-pike at them. General Wayne arrived from a party and rode among his men, promising to resolve the issue—until someone took a shot at him. Then he opened his coat.

"If you mean to kill me, shoot me at once," he cried. "Here's my heart."

This they declined to do. The mayhem continued until sometime after midnight, when the rebelling troops, "much agitated with liquor," according to one officer, marched westward to the music of fifes and drums, with fixed bayonets and a hundred head of cattle. General Wayne, unable to persuade his men to let him lead them, followed from behind, determined to keep the mutiny from spreading. He called up the local militia, sent his aide-de-camp to report on the mutiny to George Washington at his headquarters in Morristown, and ordered the New Jersey Continentals to rendezvous with them in Chatham, twelve miles away. But there was sympathy in the New Jersey camp for the Pennsylvanians, and it took the officers all night to convince the soldiers to march to Chatham.

Another drama was unfolding nearby. Tempe Wick, the captain's "buxom twenty-two-year-old daughter," in the words of a local historian, was living at home when her father died, and when her sick mother took a turn for the worse she saddled her horse and set off to fetch a doctor. History does not record what became of her mother, but the story goes that on her way back to the farm three drunken mutineers accosted Tempe, demanding her horse. In one version of the story, she told them they could have it after she rode home; in another, she pretended to dismount, and when the soldier holding the bridle let go she prodded her horse and galloped home. There she led the horse into her bedroom, tied it to the wall, slid a featherbed under its hooves to muffle any sounds, and shuttered the windows.

The soldiers, arriving soon after, searched for her horse in the barn, the outbuildings, and the woods, never thinking to check inside the house. Eventually they gave up and joined the other mutineers, who marched not to Philadelphia but to Princeton, where General Wayne would be held captive. An officer sent by Washington was not allowed to speak to the general, and it seemed that force might be necessary to end the mutiny, especially when the British caught wind of it and dispatched a pair of envoys to the Pennsylvanians, offering them bounties to switch sides. But the mutineers, refusing to follow the example of Benedict Arnold, turned the envoys over to Wayne, who summarily executed them as spies. Negotiations began, resulting, to Washington's chagrin, in a settlement conducive to the mutineers' success: some left the service with one-hundred-dollar bonuses, and others were given cash and furloughs. Months passed before the brigade was ready to fight again. Washington feared that this would set a terrible example, though his options were limited, the Pennsylvanians having remained in Princeton to underscore the risk of them deserting to the British side. He thus showed no mercy when the New Jersey line revolted, sending a detachment from New England with orders to end the insurrection by force, if necessary.

There would be no settlement this time. The New England troops surrounded the New Jersey camp, ordered their fellow colonists to parade without arms, then seized, court-martialed, and shot two ringleaders of the mutiny. "I thought it indispensable to bring the matter to an Issue and risk all extremities," Washington wrote. "Unless this dangerous spirit can be suppressed by force there is an end to all subordination in the Army, and indeed to the Army itself."

The war hung in the balance in the winter of 1781, and in my childhood I was schooled in the idea that the course of American history might have gone in a different direction if not for some decisions made in a village known to very few of my compatriots. In 1822, a local doctor wrote: "I am more than ever struck with the unparalleled measure of our sufferings, the hair-breadth escapes, the providential interpositions, and miraculous preservations, and finally the magnitude of our triumph. To me, it seems like a dream—to posterity, it must appear fabulous." So it seemed to me, for I was raised on a story—which in the manner of a dream was at once fabulous and familiar—of a war effort salvaged at its darkest point by General Wayne's inspired decision to follow his wayward troops to Princeton, by George Washington's steadiness throughout the crisis, and by the quick thinking of Tempe Wick.

I can still smell the smoke and mold in her house and the log hospital nearby, where so many soldiers died. And I remember trying to figure out how she fit her horse into the bedroom, small as it was. Her story was held up to us as a testament to her courage and ingenuity; it also offered tangible evidence that war does not spare civilians. If the version told in my childhood glossed over the mutiny, suggesting that it was the British who wanted her horse, this only instilled in me a greater taste for adventure. War loomed in my imagination.

Also politics. My first memory of our house on Cherry Lane is of climbing the dogwood tree on the chilly day in November when John F. Kennedy was buried. The televised image of a horse without a rider and a pair of boots reversed in their stirrups—a symbol, said my mother, of the slain president looking back over his life—haunted me. The soldier leading the spirited horse through the streets of the capital could not keep it from jerking at the reins, twisting from side to side as if afraid to follow the solemn procession of the flag-draped coffin. I sat for a long time on the lowest branch of the tree, trying to make sense of it all.

One overcast afternoon the next autumn, I cut a cardboard moving box in half and glued to each side photographs of Barry Goldwater clipped from *Look* and *Life* magazines, with captions like "Put Your Money Where Your Faith Is" and "In Your Heart You Know He's Right." My parents were rock-ribbed Republicans—my father, a banker who commuted to Manhattan, said he was just slightly to the left of Attila the Hun—and with this sandwich board I advertised the fact that, in Elizabeth Hard-wick's memorable phrase, I had inherited their political beliefs like flat feet. Back and forth I marched across the hill sloping from our house down to the woods, from which John Wright presently emerged. He asked me to take off my sandwich board so that he could have a closer look, and when he had laid it on the ground he removed from his pocket a penknife, with which he carefully sliced up my handiwork, explaining that my parents' candidate would *destroy* the planet, the slushy sibilant dripping from his tongue.

"All the way with LBJ," he said after reducing my political message to strips of cardboard. Then he walked back into the woods.

I was too shocked to speak or act, and now I wonder if my moral life began to take shape in that moment of paralysis. This was, I suppose, the first time anyone had challenged my family's basic view of the world. What stayed with me was John's methodical manner, his cool ferocity, which perhaps derived from the uproar over the infamous "Daisy" ad that had aired that fall for the first and only time during the network broadcast of the movie *David and Bathsheba*. A little girl counts the petals of a daisy; an adult male voice counts down from ten; a mushroom cloud from an atomic explosion fills the screen. "These are the stakes," intones President Johnson: "To make a world in which all of God's children can live, or to go into the dark. We must either love each other, or we must die." His paraphrase of the final line of W. H. Auden's "September 1, 1939" is followed by another voice, ordering viewers to vote for Johnson: "The stakes are too high for you to stay home."

John's politics must have come from his father, with whom my father feuded at zoning-commission meetings over the issue of development. The Wrights were environmentalists before it was fashionable to join the movement then in its infancy. But the publication of Rachel Carson's *Silent Spring* in 1962, the fallout from above-ground atomic-weapons testing, and the specter of apocalypse raised by the Cuban missile crisis were concentrating thinking about the fragility of nature. In our village, this took the form of Mr. Wright and others working to preserve open spaces. In 1967, land was set aside to establish Dismal Harmony, a natural area named for two brooks, Dismal and Harmony, one flowing from the reservoir, the other through a gorge: nearly 350 acres of woods and water and the remains of millraces—a space that continues to inform my dream life. For Dismal Harmony was my introduction to wilderness.

This was no wilderness in the sense of the majestic forests, deserts, and mountains of the American West, where I would spend my first years after college—lands celebrated in the works of John Muir, Wallace Stegner, Edward Abbey, and other nature writers. My wild place had been logged repeatedly over the centuries, the village of Harmony had vanished under the reservoir (no one knew the origin of the name Dismal), and I knew that if I got lost all I had to do was head downhill to find my way home. Nevertheless I felt the freedom of a frontiersman when I shuffled through the leaves to a mine, where I picked a sheet of mica from the slag and held it up to my eyes: sky, trees, and water, all turned yellow through the lens of what in the nineteenth century furnished isinglass curtains for horse-drawn carriages. On a visit to my village one recent winter day, I hiked again in Dismal Harmony, following a spur of Patriots' Path from the top of Stoney Hill Road into the woods and then blazing a trail downhill over steep terrain to arrive at a brook where, long ago, I had fished for trout.

But when it was time to return to New York I was surprised, driving slowly past our old house, to see that the dogwood was gone. Its absence pierced my heart.

Dismal Harmony's current plant list includes different varieties of maple, hickory, birch, and oak, as well as red cedar, tulip, Norway spruce, American basswood and beech, blackberry and butternut. No dogwoods. For the native dogwood, *Cornus florida*, what some call an "altar tree" of American forests, with its white or pink flowers and scarlet berries, is another casualty of human interference with nature, its numbers in the last decades having radically diminished for reasons detailed below. In an interview about her book *The Sixth Extinction*, Elizabeth Kolbert noted that "the prevailing view of change on planet Earth, as one paleontologist put it, is that the history of life consists of long periods of boredom interrupted occasionally by panic"—a variation on the old adage about war, the subject of several books of mine. The empty spot where my dogwood tree once stood brought home to me the fact that in addition to our inordinate fondness for shaping history by military means we are also adept at waging war on nature.

Evolution is the story of adaptation to changing circumstances, and if I once imagined my life as an act of revolt against authority I have come to see it now as a sequence of accommodations in the key of war, the first battles of which were played out in my childhood. In *Biophilia: The Human Bond with Other Species*, Edward

O. Wilson suggests that "it is possible to spend a lifetime in a magellanic voyage around the trunk of a single tree." What follows is an account of the journey I have made around the dogwood at the edge of our land.

Names

The dogwood's etymology is murky. One theory holds that the name descends from the Old English word for dagger, the wood being hard enough to fashion into goads and arrows as well as skewers and spindles. It furnished shuttles for the textile industry, which flourished in our village until the Civil War, when, as Kelby Ouchley notes in *Flora and Fauna of the Civil War*, the wood was used for "charcoal, engraving, mallets, tool handles, wedges, plane stock, harrow teeth, hames [the curved pieces of a harness], horse collars, ox yokes, wheel hubs, barrel hoops, machinery bearings, and cogs in various types of gears." Also gunpowder and toothpicks. There was no connection to dogs in the origin of the name, the canine element emerging only with a change in the language, when the *a* in *dag* became an *o*. Dog-tree, Dog-berry, Dog-timber, Houndberry—these names were coined, possibly because the bark was said to make "an excellent wash for mangy dogs," or because of the barking sound created by branches rubbing together in the wind. Dogberry was the name Shakespeare gave to a foolish constable in *Much Ado about Nothing*, and it thus became a symbol of ignorant officials wielding power injudiciously. (Has the time come to bestow this name on certain American politicians?) It so happened that my family bred English springer spaniels, which I associate with the tree, for I saw my father cry only twice in my childhood: once when his father died, and again when the last puppy in a litter was stillborn, a handful of wet brown fur that he buried by the dogwood.

The nomenclature is complicated, but there are roughly sixty species of dogwood in the world, the majority of them in the northern hemisphere, including ground covers, shrubs, and trees. In *Dogwoods*, the definitive guide to the species that are available in nurseries, Paul Cappiello and Don Shadow suggest that the tree was "central to the march of civilization," since wood from *Cornus mas*, the dogwood native to southern Europe, Iran, the Levant, and other parts of Eurasia, was supposedly used to build the Trojan horse, the fabulous contraption in which Odysseus and his men hid while the rest of the Greek forces pretended to sail home. Virgil recounts in

The Aeneid how one warrior, Sinon, stays behind, ostensibly forgotten by his fellow Greeks; in fact he has been ordered to convince the Trojans to accept the horse as an offering. After ten bloody years of war, the Trojans, refusing to heed Laocoön's warning to beware of Greeks bearing gifts, fall for the ruse, drag the horse into the city, and then launch a victory celebration, which continues into the night, until they finally sink into a drunken stupor. Then Sinon opens the hatch in the horse so that Odysseus and his men, armed with arrows made from dogwood branches, can head to the city gate to let in the returning Greeks, who proceed to slaughter their sleeping enemies.

The European dogwood, also known as the cornelian cherry, is probably too small to have supplied planks for the Trojan horse. But the wood is elastic and hard enough to lend credence to the story that the Greeks' weapons were made from it; the classics scholar Minor M. Markle III argues that for centuries it was "prized as the best material for spears, javelins, and bows." Philip II of Macedon used it to create the sarissa, the long double-pointed pike central to the success of the phalanx, the infantry formation that changed the nature of warfare. By the time his son Alexander the Great began his conquest, Markle writes, "the name of the wood was used in poetry as a synonym for spear."

Cornus means "of the horn" and is related to the Latin words for tusk, the horns of the crescent moon, the wing of an army, a musical instrument played by Roman soldiers, the end of a book or scroll, power, strength, might. Elizabeth Bishop's poem "Florida" begins, "The state with the prettiest name." The same holds for the botanical name of the dogwood native to the eastern United States, *Cornus florida*, which may be translated as "flowering horn." It is surely one of the prettiest trees in forests and backyards from Maine to Florida and westward to Illinois—a small nesting tree, rarely more than forty feet tall, with opposite or adjacent pairs of oval leaves and clusters of what botanists call perfect inconspicuous yellow flowers, surrounded by four white or pink petal-like leaves known as bracts. Its bark, ridged and broken, is said to resemble the hide of an alligator (my first calluses date from climbing our dogwood). White-tailed deer and rabbits feed on its twigs and leaves, and in the fall its scarlet fruit, which is mildly poisonous to humans, provides food for squirrels, foxes, beavers, skunks, and black bears, as well as thirty-six species of birds, including bobwhites, cardinals, cedar waxwings, robins, mockingbirds, wild turkeys, and woodpeckers.

It is an understory tree, which grows in the shade of the forest canopy, and since it attracts songbirds you could say that it inspires music. Language, too. Linguists posit that sometime in the last hundred thousand years our ancestors began to imitate birdsong and monkey alarm calls in delight, boredom, or terror, depending on the circumstances; the fusion of these two finite systems of communication from the animal world produced a third system, seemingly infinite, capable of conveying holistic messages. The integration hypothesis of human language evolution proposes that the combination of avian music and primate warning, the expressive and lexical layers of meaning, gave rise to grammar, and the rest is history—which is to say, the history of speech. The invention of language made possible what we imagine to comprise human experience, for good or ill—agriculture, warfare, religion, government, poetry, philosophy, art, and science, not to mention the emotions that drive individuals, societies, and civilizations. Long ago, under a tree, we learned to express ourselves in a new key, building structures of meaning word by word, phrase by phrase, alert to the necessities of living, to the varieties of love and grief, to the mysteries of faith, quirks of nature, and consolations of storytelling. Just as speech disorders may dissolve in singing, so did our stuttering attempts to make sense of our walk in the sun come together with the addition of birdsong to our repertoire; the musical possibilities encoded in language expanded our understanding of the worlds without and within, giving birth to poetry—and so much more.

The growing silence in eastern North American hardwood forests, a function of the decline of native dogwoods, may thus be an augur of our fate, for a report published in *Science* suggests that climate change and loss of biosphere integrity jeopardize our very existence. Researchers, building on the concept of planetary boundaries, an earth-system framework constructed to define the environmental limits within which humanity can safely operate, have concluded that as a result of human activity four of the nine boundaries have been breached. After the Ice Age, relatively stable environmental conditions marked life on earth for 11,700 years, in what scientists refer to as the Holocene epoch, fostering the development of human civilization, which spread across the earth and into space. But in the last century, with the effects of the Industrial Revolution reaching everywhere, this stable order has shown signs of dissolving, with rising temperatures and sea levels, melting icepacks in the Arctic and Antarctica, the depletion of the ozone layer, the destruction of native habitats, and agricultural runoff adding enough nitrogen and phosphorous to our waterways to create nearly 150 ecological dead zones, from the Baltic Sea to Lake Erie to the Gulf of Mexico.

"It might be possible for human civilization to live outside Holocene conditions, but it's never been tried before," said Steve Carpenter, one of eighteen members of the research team that produced the study "Planetary Boundaries: Guiding Human Development on a Changing Planet." Carpenter hoped this research would serve as a wake-up call for policy makers. But history is awash in examples of societies dismissing warnings of impending disaster until it is too late to change course. Foresight is a function of clear thinking, and clarity is in demand now more than ever. If in poetry I learned a way to come to terms with the fallout from the governing emotion of my childhood—the fear of corporal punishment administered by my parents—and then to see into the life of things, I turn now to nature to measure the limits of my blinkered vision and to reconcile my fear of loss on an infinitely larger scale.

In the spring of my ninth year, while recuperating from surgery to correct my crossed eyes, I spent the better part of two weeks playing outside. If only my friends could see me with an eye patch, I thought as I sailed like a pirate aboard the blossoming dogwood, running my fingers over the bark, chewing on twigs, squinting through the leaves at the changing patterns of clouds. This was my second eye operation in two years, mandated by my stubborn refusal to do the vision-therapy exercises prescribed by the ophthalmologist. I hated staring at the kaleidoscope of blurry figures displayed inside a cardboard box, trying to make my eyes fuse; after going under the knife again, I became resigned to using one eye. But what I saw in the dogwood stayed with me—the ridges in the bark, the play of light on the notched white bracts, the yellow petals of the flowers. This was when I began to learn the language of trees.

Questions of Belief

The legend that Jesus was crucified on a cross made of dogwood, derived from a popular poem, persists in part because the anonymous writer paid close attention to the physical characteristics of the tree, discerning in them a comprehensive set of symbols: the bracts form a cross, one pair longer than the other, that is notched as if by nails, bearing red or brown spots like fresh or dried blood; the cluster of flowers brings to mind the crown of thorns bestowed on the Son of Man; the twisted, slender trunk is a token of his promise that henceforth the dogwood will never grow large enough to be used as an instrument of torture and death: "this tree shall be / A reminder to all of My agony." Three days after the Passion, the wood gatherer who supplied the cross discovers that all the trees in the dogwood grove are withering. Years pass before bushes sprout in the wasteland, with blossoms that look as if they were burned by a cross. It is also said that the pink dogwood blushes in shame over the innocent blood it shed.

Biblical accounts of the Crucifixion do not mention any dogwoods. Indeed the only cross excavated in Jerusalem likely came from an olive tree. A similar provenance is suggested by analysis of some of the thousands of pieces of the True Cross allegedly discovered by Constantine's mother, Helena; distributed to monasteries and churches throughout Christendom (enough to fill a ship, John Calvin remarked); and venerated by Roman Catholic and Orthodox Christians. *Cornus mas* may have grown in Palestine when Jesus lived and died, and since an eye schooled in faith sees what it wants to see (the Psalms begin with the assertion that the faithful man "shall be like a tree planted by the rivers of water, that brings forth its fruit in its season, whose leaf shall not wither"), it is no surprise that for Christians the sight of dogwoods blossoming at Easter can reinforce the message of the Passion and the Resurrection, even if it does not confirm the legend.

Such folk beliefs may elicit scorn from the scientific community, though ethnobotanists exploring traditional uses of plants understand that indigenous forms of knowledge may have contemporary applications. Professor David T. Thomas observes that the dogwood is ranked fifth among plants in North America for the number of uses Native peoples found for it—nearly two hundred in all, primarily medicinal. The bark, when chewed, can alleviate fevers and pains, head- and toothaches, ailments of the kidneys, lungs, stomach, and throat. Some tribes dried the inner bark to make dyes or mixed it with tobacco leaves to smoke in sacred pipes; some wove the fiber into baskets; some brushed their teeth with twigs. During the Civil War, Confederate doctors used the bark as a substitute for quinine in the treatment of malaria. And in Chinese medicine it is prescribed for arthritis, while the fruits are made into an astringent tonic for those afflicted with impotence, lumbago, vertigo, and night sweats.

I take a more-than-passing interest in such wisdom since being diagnosed with rheumatoid arthritis, an incurable disease that also afflicts my father. It is unnerving to watch his decline (his deformed joints, his failing kidneys), not least because it may herald my own fate. Ever since the fall of 1968, when he was confined to bed for months with a mysterious illness, I have had the strange sense that his health and mine are linked. My family had rented a cottage that year on the hill behind the Brookside Community Church, and as soon as I got home from school I would go outside to kick a soccer ball against the cement wall leading to the garage. The leaves of the dog-wood tree to my left, outside my parents' bedroom, were turning red, the steeple at eye level to my right glinted in the sun, and when I juggled the ball I looked out the corner of each eye, now at the tree, now at the steeple, fig-uring that if my eyes would not fuse, then I could develop my peripheral vision: an athletic necessity, according to my friends. When I grew tired of that, I walked to the edge of the hill and waited for the church bell to toll across the chasm of air. It was better to stay outside than risk my mother's wrath. Construction on our new house was be-hind schedule, and she was easily aggravated.

In my recurring nightmare—derived from a photo-graph in a magazine of soldiers carrying a shirtless pris-oner through a swamp in Vietnam, his hands and feet bound to a bamboo pole, like a fish reeled in from the sea—I was the POW, and when I awoke in a cold sweat, trembling from head to toe, unable to breathe under my covers, I did not dare wake my parents, who were sleeping downstairs. My mother warned my sisters and me not to disturb my father.

The war was coming closer. As the hours of daylight dwindled, I would watch the nightly news with my father, who paid close attention to the stories from Vietnam. On

New Year's Day, 1969, my baseball coach's nephew, Robert Tufts, began his tour of duty in Quang Ngai Province; at the end of the month the Tet Offensive began, with the Viet Cong launching surprise attacks throughout South Vietnam; and when later that winter Sam Tufts, Robert's uncle and our plumber, came to fix a clogged toilet he muttered something to my mother about the progress of the war, which did not interest me. I wanted to hear him talk about baseball.

I could not wait for the spring day when my father would be well enough to pitch batting practice to me. What success I had in Little League was no guarantee that at the next level, the Babe Ruth League, I would even make the team, not with my eyesight. Yet when that day arrived I ignored my father's instructions to choke up on the bat so as to improve my chances of making contact, and for some reason I stroked one line drive after another, my confidence growing with each hit, the sweet sound of connecting with each pitch ringing in my ears, until he realized that I was disobeying him. Infuriated, he ordered me to choke up, and when I refused he threw a fastball at my head. I ducked; the ball rattled the cage; my father stormed off the field, rubbing his arm. He never pitched to me again. Nor did I ever again see the ball as well as I did that day. I fell into a slump that lasted through the season, which ended not long before the Fourth of July celebration, the high point of the summer.

Everyone turned out for the parade, which usually started at the juncture of Tingley Road and Main Street, sometimes backing up to Dogwood Drive, and wended for half a mile through the shade of maple trees to the center of Brookside. There would be marching bands and volunteer firefighters from all the surrounding towns, scout troops, Little Leaguers, the local 4-H club, horseback riders and bicyclists, politicians and police. Carpenters would compete with one another to build the most elaborate float (another reason why our house remained unfinished), and by the time the procession passed the church and bank and turned at the post office to circle the white clapboard community club the noise would be general. Everyone would stand for the prayer and the singing of the national anthem, and then the contests would begin on the baseball field—a turtle race, a frog jump (every year on the eve of the parade my father and I would track the mating calls of bullfrogs in the swamp off Combs Hollow Road until we caught one), flour blowing, watermelon eating, and ladder raising, which our fire department always won. Sam Tufts, who was also the fire chief, would hold the ladder for Ernie Maw, a carpenter who would climb to the top faster than anybody else and ring the bell loud enough to wake Creation. Horseshoe pitching would follow, and skeet shooting, and a senior-league baseball game, where you could count on Sam Tufts hitting one over the fence.

Robert Tufts stepped on a land mine three weeks before the parade in 1969. News of his death traveled quickly, thanks in part to my mother, who invoked Sam Tufts's name in nearly every phone conversation. Sam must have missed some baseball practices, though I do not remember him being absent from the field, and on the Fourth he marched with the firefighters in his customary white T-shirt and green trousers. He climbed the steps of the community club to join my father and other dignitaries on the reviewing stand, and that was when my friend Bobby Courtet suggested that we head back to his house to watch the rest of the parade.

It was a warm, humid morning, with sunlight filtering through the leaves of the trees lining the road, and from the front porch I heard a siren dying far away. Tricycles passed, and Cub Scouts, and a red convertible filled with veterans from World War II. My mother was explaining something to Mrs. Courtet when an ominous silence descended suddenly over everything. Even my mother stopped talking to look down the road, toward the sound of a muffled drum coming our way. A funeral cortege appeared at the bend in the curve, with four hooded figures dressed all in black carrying a pasteboard coffin on their shoulders. No one said a word as they marched slowly past, the drumbeat as insistent as it was jarring. Bobby tapped me on the shoulder when the protesters were almost out of sight, and we took off to follow them.

At the community club, they distributed leaflets detailing their opposition to the war, some of which were torn up by a neighbor, and then they sat down in the outfield. A crowd milled around them during the prayer. When they did not stand for the singing of "The Star-Spangled Banner," Sam Tufts dragged them to their feet, yanking off their hoods. Something snapped in our grieving coach when one protester took exception to the rough treatment. He wrapped his large hands around the teenager's throat to choke him, growling that he was a traitor. In fact the local draft board had declared the boy 4-F, sparing him military service. Another protester went on to become a modestly successful poet, who later wrote about the fear he felt that day. I do not recall if Sam Tufts got any hits in the senior-league game.

Cain and Abel

"Good morning, trees," my friend called out as we sped by the blossoming dogwoods. It was not much after dawn, cold and drizzling, and when I asked him to roll his window up he held out his arm as if to run his fingers through the branches. I accelerated into the curve at the top of the hill, and on the way down I asked him once again. He folded his arms on the sill, resting his chin in his hands, and wept. "It's so beautiful," he said, tears streaming down his face.

The daily drama of our commute to the Pingry School in Hillside had reached a new level of absurdity. A. was never ready when I got to his house, his father was threatening to kick him out if he did not pull himself together, and my physics teacher had marked me tardy fifty-seven days in a row. When I failed the physics midterm, the guidance counselor let me drop the course on the condition that I see a therapist about "the situation," which in my mind could be reduced to a simple equation: my friend was going crazy, and no one seemed to want to help him.

The drive to school took an hour, from the woods of Jockey Hollow to the edge of the Great Swamp, past a pharmaceutical company in Summit that employed some of our classmates' parents and the social club in Union that sponsored our team in the German-American soccer league, and over the course of several months I witnessed radical changes in my friend, a brilliant student, artist, and soccer player who was becoming delusional. The outlandish things he said and did in the early stages of his illness—he once ran twelve miles to visit his girlfriend in Morristown, then hid his sneakers under a bush in front of her house to obscure the pains he had taken to see her—stopped being funny the fall of his senior year, after he led Pingry to the state championship, soccer being his last tether to reality. By winter, his psychosis was apparent to everyone at school. Why his family did not seek help for him was a mystery.

What was most unnerving about A.'s descent into madness was that it coincided with his efforts to tutor me about the meaning of life, beginning with the novels of Hermann Hesse, Kurt Vonnegut, and Richard Brautigan. A. was a year ahead of me in school, far more popular than I could ever hope to be, and at first our commute was a thrilling artistic and intellectual journey, a time to explore themes and ideas in *Beneath the Wheel*, *Slaughterhouse-Five*, and *Trout Fishing in America*—the alienation of a gifted student, the horror of war, the lure of the counterculture. Our mantra came from Brautigan's *A Confederate General from Big Sur*: "He was reading the Russians with that certain heavy tone people put in their voices when they say, 'I'm reading the Russians.'" We listened to eight-track tapes of Fairport Convention and The Band, Renaissance and a folk duo called Aztec Two-Step; debated the merits of Bob Dylan, Nietzsche, and *Monty Python's Flying Circus*; shared what we were reading about utopian communities—the Shakers, the Amish, the Merry Pranksters. The draft had ended, Watergate and the fall of Saigon lay in the future, and for a newly licensed driver like me the world seemed rich with possibility.

A recurring theme for us was the conflict between illusion and reality embodied in *Demian*, Hesse's bildungsroman composed toward the end of World War I. The carnage compelled Hesse to write antiwar tracts, and a cascading series of personal losses—his father died, his son fell seriously ill, his wife suffered a mental breakdown—colored his first major novel, which was also the first novel to profoundly shape my thinking. From the opening words—"I wanted only to try to live in accord with the promptings which came from my true self. Why was that so very difficult?"—I felt as if Hesse were confiding in me. In the narrator's recollection of an unsettling afterschool encounter with his classmate Demian, whose interpretation of the Cain and Abel story contradicts the narrator's understanding of it—Cain's mark in this telling being a sign of strength and courage instead of God's curse—I experienced the shiver of recognition that fiction can inspire. I shared the narrator's unease, having imbibed a traditional reading of the story in confirmation class, and since I secretly feared that the tree-shaped scar on my forehead, courtesy of a fall as a toddler from the kitchen counter with a glass in my hand, was a sign of kinship with Cain, I thought Hesse had built an invisible bridge from his imagination to mine. Nothing grew from the earth on which Abel's blood had been shed; no one could harm Cain without provoking God's wrath; and the descendants of the first murderer named in history were condemned to drown in the flood. Not that one had to commit a grievous crime to be cast out, as A.'s increasingly erratic behavior showed. My own adolescent sense of alienation from my family and classmates brought me closer to A., who in his rare moments of lucidity seemed to possess some of Demian's gifts of wisdom and foresight. I had a premonition that my fate was bound to his, disastrous as that might be.

Late in the novel, Demian's mother, Eva, who also bears the sign of Cain, tells the narrator a story about a young man in love with a star: how one night he stood on a high cliff above the seashore, gazing in longing at the star, and leaped into space to meet it. But at that moment he thought, "It is impossible! And so he was dashed to pieces on the rocks below. He did not know how to love. Had he had the strength of soul, at the moment of leaping, to believe in the fulfillment of his wish, he would have flown up and have been united with the star." The narrator, Sinclair, is in love with Eva, whom he calls Mother Eve, and she promises to come to him if he can win her love. When Sinclair makes a silent inward petition to her, Demian arrives to say that war is coming. "Dear Sinclair," she tells him at dinner that night, "you called me today. You know why I did not come myself. But don't forget, you know the call now and if you ever need someone who bears the sign, call me again." This he does in the last scene. He is on sentry duty at the front, thinking of her and Demian, and then he is vouchsafed a vision in the clouds of a large city, from which rises the figure of a god with the features of Mother Eve. Suddenly she cries out in pain, and from her forehead spring stars, one of which rushes through the night to meet him—a shell bursting into a thousand sparks. Severely wounded, he is taken to a cellar, then to a stable, and then on a stretcher, a mysterious force drawing him onward, calling him, until one night, fully conscious, he finds himself in a room, lying next to Demian, who explains that he must heed the voice inside him. "And one more thing: Mother Eve said that if ever you were ill I was to give you a kiss from her, which she gave me. . . . Close your eyes, Sinclair!" Demian kisses him—on his lips there is a trace of blood, "which never seemed to stop flowing"—and then he falls asleep. On waking in the morning he thinks, "The bandaging hurt me. All that has happened to me since hurt me." *Amen*, I said, closing the book.

It occurs to me that A.'s exclamation over the flowering dogwoods that morning may have been prompted by Hesse's *Wandering: Notes and Sketches*, which appeared in 1920. After the war, the grieving writer settled in a mountain village in Switzerland, determined, as he wrote to a friend, "to live as a hermit in nature and in my work." What emerged was a series of meditations on the land in prose, poetry, and watercolor, which taught generations to see into the depths of the natural world. One essay begins, "Trees are sanctuaries. Whoever knows how to speak to them, whoever knows how to listen to them, can learn the truth. They do not preach learning and precepts, they preach, undeterred by particulars, the ancient law of life." How to obey that law? It is the task of a lifetime to learn to heed the truth. Perhaps A. thought that if he listened to trees, really listened, they might heal his madness. On we drove to school.

It is difficult to pinpoint the moment when my friend's unconventional behavior began to raise alarms. He was not the only student at Pingry loath to brush his teeth, bathe, or change his clothes. Nor was he alone in his taste for illicit drugs. His flights of fancy, which provided me with plenty of comic material, I attributed to the amount of pot and hash he smoked, until it dawned on me that he said crazy things even when he was straight. The joke at school was that because in one soccer match he had the most touches on the ball—contacts, in soccer parlance—he had a contact high. He played the state tournament stoned out of his mind, and sometime in the winter of 1974, inspired by Carlos Castaneda's *The Teachings of Don Juan: A Yaqui Way of Knowledge*, he began to experiment with mescaline and psilocybin mushrooms.

Was that what sent him over the edge? I have asked myself that question for forty years.

Unaccountably, he decided to run track that spring, specializing in distance events. Though he regularly skipped practice, it was not long after his revelation about the beauty of dogwoods that he somehow qualified for the state championship in the two-mile race. He adopted an unusual strategy for the race, taking off on his final sprint after only the first of eight laps, drawing so far ahead of the other runners that from the infield of the track his coach ordered him to slow down, waving his arms frantically, to no avail. A. was on pace to set a high school record in the event, maybe even a world record, well under nine minutes. He was more than a lap ahead of the next competitor, with less than a hundred yards to go, and still he did not let up. Faster and faster he ran, until he collapsed thirty yards from the finish line. He came in last.

"What were you thinking?" I asked him the next morning on the way to school.

"I was running and running and running," he explained, kneading his thighs with both hands, "and then my legs told me they couldn't run anymore."

I tried to avoid him after graduation, unwilling to be distracted from my own pursuits (girls, drugs, writing)—

which made the last news I had of him all the harder to bear. He flunked out of college and drifted for the next few years from place to place, now bunking with friends until he wore out his welcome, now undergoing treatment in a psychiatric hospital. One night he used a razor blade to castrate himself—and survived. My aunt, who was one of the emergency medical technicians called to the scene, did not want to talk about what she had witnessed. The inquiries I made about him over the years yielded little useful information. One friend heard him call in to a late-night radio program in New York, eliciting from the host a bemused reaction to his wild theories and non sequiturs. Another suggested that he had solved all his problems at a stroke, a malicious idea that may contain an element of truth. But for me his act of self-destruction remains inexplicable. And what cannot be explained may become fertile ground for not only gossip and speculation but mythmaking: say that the spots of red on dogwood blossoms issue from the blood spattered by my friend, in what must have been unendurable agony.

Some Mohawk communities believe that in the Sky World the dogwood is the Tree of Life. In another Native American tale, the gods, angered by a chief's excessive demands for gifts from the suitors of his four daughters, changed him into a dogwood, his daughters now attending on him in the form of bracts. And then there are the indigenous stories about little people living in the woods, like gnomes and fairies and leprechauns: the Dogwood People, dreamers and seekers of harmony. Delicate, physically and emotionally, they stay invisible unless they choose to reveal themselves in the spring. Then they take a look around, and their tears become dogwood blossoms, which linger on the trees only when we treat nature and one another well. The Cherokees think these spirits were sent here to protect infants, care for the old and sick, and teach us to help others out of the goodness of our hearts, not in the expectation of personal gain. The names of five dogwood varieties begin with *Cherokee*—Daybreak, Chief, Brave, Princess, and Sunset—in honor of the Dogwood People. Call A. an honorary member of that tribe.

Woeful Predicament

William Bartram (1739–1823), the first notable American-born naturalist, recorded in his *Travels through North and South Carolina, Georgia, East and West Florida, the Cherokee Country, . . .* a description of dogwoods in one of Alabama's "grand high forests," in the summer of 1775, that may leave contemporary readers grieving over the loss of our natural abundance:

> We now entered a very remarkable grove of Dog wood
> trees (Cornus Florida), which continued nine or ten miles
> unalterable, except here and there a towering Magnolia
> grandiflora; the land on which they stand is an exact level:
> the surface a shallow, loose, black mould, on a stratum
> of stiff, yellowish clay; these trees were about twelve feet
> high, spreading horizontally; their limbs meeting and
> interlocking with each other, formed one vast, shady, cool
> grove, so dense and humid as to exclude the sun-beams,

and prevent the intrusion of almost every other vegetable, affording us a most desirable shelter from the fervid sun-beams at noon-day. This admirable grove by way of eminence has acquired the name of the Dog woods.

He continues through this forest for nearly seventy miles, unaware that his fellow colonists are waging war against the British, and passes more dogwood groves, imagining that in spring the trees, "when covered with blossoms, present a most pleasing scene; when at the same time a variety of other sweet shrubs display their beauty"—and then he catalogues their names, Halesia and Stewartia and Azalea and more, concluding with a vision of "the superb Magnolia grandiflora, standing in front of the dark groves, towering far above the common level."

Bartram's environmental classic, which mixes lavish descriptions of flora and fauna with astute observations about Cherokee, Choctaw, Creek, and Seminole Indians, inspired Samuel Taylor Coleridge's dream of founding a utopian community of poets and philosophers in America and contributed to some of the imagery in Coleridge's fantasia "Kubla Khan." Bartram himself cut a romantic figure as the impractical artistic son of a famous botanist. Indeed he failed at several business enterprises, incurring substantial debts (paid off by his father, who subsequently deeded his profitable garden to William's younger brother), and when he set out from Philadelphia in 1773 on a four-year expedition through the southern colonies he must have relished his newfound freedom. With funding from a family friend, he covered 2,400 miles, collected hundreds of plant specimens, made scores of drawings; by the time he published *Travels* in 1791, he had secured subscriptions for the book from founding fathers such as George Washington, John Adams, and Thomas Jefferson, the latter of whom later invited him to join an expedition in the Louisiana Territory. (He declined.)

Though only one American edition of the book appeared in his lifetime, along with several foreign editions, it had an immediate effect on scientific thought. Many leading naturalists retraced his route through the South, including Thomas Nuttall and John James Audubon, as did the English geologist Sir Charles Lyell, who, according to the Bartram Trail Conference, used Bartram's descriptions of cliffs and alluvial plains to support his theory "that all geological phenomena could be explained as the result of existing forces operating uniformly through time"—a theory that shaped Darwin's thinking about evolution. Bartram taught Alexander Wilson to identify and draw birds, for which the author of the seven-volume *American Ornithology* gave him full credit: "[My pictures] may yet tell posterity that I was honored with your friendship," he wrote to Bartram in 1805, "and that to your inspiration they owe their existence." Audubon's desire to outdo Wilson, painting all the birds of North America, betrays the same fervor to possess comprehensive knowledge of the natural world that fueled Bartram's *Travels*; *The Birds of America* includes prints of dozens of new species Audubon discovered, as well as at least six more that have since gone extinct. Bartram's friendship with Wilson thus taught us how to see the world.

Consider Bartram's description of the dogwood grove, whose salient feature is that it offers shelter from the sun. In these pages Bartram plays down his Quakerism—during the Revolutionary War, when much of his book was written, Quakers were suspected of harboring Tory sympathies—but the intellectual curiosity, respect for others, and humility associated with the Society of Friends mark every page of his *Travels*. Take the story of his encounter with a Seminole warrior who, wronged by a white man, resolves to kill the next white man he meets— only to become friends with the explorer. Bartram was a congenial man, and, like his father—who freed his slaves, taught them to read and write, shared meals with them—he had an abiding concern for human rights. Delegates to the Constitutional Convention in Philadelphia in 1787, including Alexander Hamilton, James Madison, and George Mason, visited his garden, and as he showed them around they must have discussed their deliberations about the terms of the American experiment in liberty. It is tempting to imagine history taking a different course, if Bartram's ideas about equality had ended up in our founding documents. "God is no respector of Persons," he wrote in an address to Congress. "The Black, White, Red and Yellow People are equally dear to him and under his protection and favour. . . . Do we not continue in a woefull predicament by suffering the Black People who are fellow citizens of our Nation to be held in perpetual Bondage and slavery?"

The legacy of this "woefull predicament" shaped my experience of the South, which dated from my freshman year in college. My family had moved to Raleigh, North Carolina, the previous summer, my father having left his job in New York to reorganize a failing bank, and it was clear to them, if not to me, that in the wake of losing my home I was adrift. Their new house lay in the shade of dogwoods, and under ordinary circumstances I might have welcomed the sight of familiar trees when I traveled there for Easter, not to mention my mother's cooking. But I had gotten into trouble in New Jersey over Christmas break, the repercussions from which would change my life. What happened was this. On my way back to Middlebury, I had stopped in Brookside to see friends, particularly a raven-haired field-hockey player who had inflamed my imagination for as long as I could remember. One night, driving her home from a party, drunk and stoned on screwdrivers and pot, I had the feeling that her interest in me was growing, until a squad car appeared in the rearview mirror. She remained calm, and as we rounded a curve she threw a plastic bag of pot out the window—which was when the police pulled us over. They found the contraband in no time at all, and in the glare of the police station, where we were booked, photographed, and fingerprinted—to the amusement of the friends we called to bail us out—I saw from the expression on her face that in addition to our legal problems I had no hope now of winning her hand. In fact I never saw her again after our single court appearance, which at our lawyer's request was closed to the public (we were, after all, from prominent families, and white). The judge accepted our guilty pleas, fined us $250 apiece, and sentenced us to six months' probation; if we stayed out of trouble, he said, our records would be expunged within the year. I said good-bye to my partner in crime and returned to school. My parents ordered me to spend my next vacation at home.

Rembrandt's *Return of the Prodigal Son* had made a deep impression on me in a survey of art history during my first semester, and I approached my Easter home-coming in something of the same spirit as the lost soul rendered with such exquisite care by the Dutchman. My mother and I stayed up late on the night of my arrival to discuss what I had done and how I might redeem my-self—a heart-to-heart conversation that stopped short of forgiveness but that nonetheless was for me an unburden-ing. I slept soundly that night for the first time in weeks, and upon waking in the morning I decided to go for a run. There were blossoming dogwoods on every street (*Cornus florida* is the state flower of both North Carolina and Vir-ginia), and as I ran in the brisk spring air, grateful for the reprieve from the harsh Vermont winter, I felt a sudden burst of freedom, which gave me the idea to keep going for more than an hour. I sprinted the last hundred yards to our driveway, and then sat under a dogwood to cool down.

Once inside the house, though, a strange sensation came over me. My lips, the backs of my thighs, the surgical scars on my knee and belly—all swelled and itched. My tongue thickened, and it was difficult to swallow. I was breaking out in hives, which quickly spread over my entire body; as soon as I finished scratching one place, another patch of skin flared. When my breathing grew labored, I panicked. Our family doctor, unable to determine the cause of my reaction over the phone, assured my mother that there was no reason to worry—though my hives did not fade for hours, leaving me utterly spent. Over time I would associate this episode with the dogwood, regarded by some Native American tribes in the South as a symbol of protection. Had I reacted to it? All I knew was that I had returned to the shelter of my family to sort out some complicated things in my life, and within hours I literally could not breathe.

On the night before I went back to Middlebury, my father announced that he had lined up a summer job for me at a client's lumberyard, where in his words I would learn the value of hard work. This was an understatement. When I returned to Raleigh in late May, the temperature and humidity were in the nineties, and on my first morning of work I sweated through my T-shirt in a matter of minutes, heaving onto a pickup truck bags of cement that weighed nearly a hundred pounds apiece. More contractors backed into the loading dock, each bearing an order for thirty or more bags of cement, and since they were in a hurry I did not slow down for two hours, despite the fact that I had long since stopped sweating. After the last truck pulled away, the foreman sent me to the brick pile, and for the rest of the morning I used a rusted pair of tongs to pick up ten bricks at a time and carry them some distance to a flatbed truck, which was scheduled to make a delivery after lunch. It did not seem possible to survive such a regimen.

The foreman, one of four whites in a workforce of more than two hundred, took a dim view of me, not because I had gotten into trouble (he employed several ex-cons) but because I was a college student from the North. His jokes about my education had an edge: Did your professors teach you to punch a time card? In my presence he liked to remind the other whites—an old farmer recovering from a stroke, a taciturn driver, and a high school dropout who was planning to join the Ku Klux Klan—that Yankees were unreliable. It would be a long summer.

Work ended early on Fridays, at two o'clock, and one week the foreman ordered me to stay until five with a lanky forklift operator named Charlie Ed, who had worked in the lumberyard for more than twenty years. Charlie Ed sat on a wooden pallet piled high with bags of cement, took a swig from a flask of vodka, and passed it to me. I wondered aloud if there was orange juice in the vending machine. He let out a laugh, then advised me to drink it straight.

"If you cut it with anything," he explained, "you can't tell how much you're drinking."

I followed his lead—and ended up drunk. I also gained more understanding of our common heritage than what I had absorbed in a year of American history lectures at Middlebury. Charlie Ed spoke without rancor about the difficulties of raising a family on $3.20 an hour, which was not much more than what I earned, and since I barely saved a penny, despite the fact that my parents provided my food and shelter, I could not imagine how he survived. From a seam in my memory rose the smell of burning wood from the clouds of smoke and ash that in the summer of 1967 had drifted over Brookside from fires set in Newark's race riots. What had heretofore been an abstraction—the disenfranchisement of African Americans—took on a tangible quality in the stories Charlie Ed told of his regular run-ins with the police. He was, I realized belatedly, instructing me in the ways of the world; from that day forward he interceded on my behalf whenever the foreman made an unreasonable request.

After work, I would train at a nearby soccer field, determined to make Middlebury's varsity team, running sprints in the muggy air, juggling the ball, practicing set pieces, shooting on goal, and then I would read myself to sleep—which rarely took long. I had no social life to speak of, until a high school friend arranged a blind date for me with a girl from Sweet Briar. She spent the evening extolling the virtues of her purity, leading me to believe I had no hope of scoring with her, only to throw herself at me as soon as I parked the car in her driveway. I could not help giggling, and when she asked what was so funny I mentioned her purity, which in the event turned out to be less important than I had figured. But when I showed up for our next date in a T-shirt and jeans, she excused herself to change out of her dress into cutoffs and a blouse, plainly miffed at my casual style. On the way to the movie theater she asked how work had gone with "the sawmill niggers." I gave her a look, which inspired another question: "Don't they smell different?" I wish I could say we did not get together again, but I was lonely.

This was the summer of the bicentennial, and as I drove north for the Fourth of July weekend the unfinished business of the American Revolution was much on my mind. The traffic outside Washington, D.C., slowed my progress; to distract myself, I tried to imagine the lives of my coworkers: Charlie Ed, and a sawyer who had served twenty-six years in prison, and a driver unimpaired by his hourly stop for a beer. But the gulf between us was too wide for me to bridge. I arrived at my grandmother's house in Brookside in a foul mood. Early on Sunday morning I made my way to New York City, where some friends from high school were drinking mimosas on the roof of an apartment building in lower Manhattan, watching a regatta of tall ships sail around New York Harbor. An international fleet of warships saluted the USS *Wainwright*, the guided missile cruiser carrying President Gerald Ford, and with each report we downed another glass. My speech was slurred by the time I started driving south late in the afternoon; as the hours passed, my eyelids grew heavier and heavier. Near midnight, I crossed the border into North Carolina, listening to George Harrison sing "While My Guitar Gently Weeps" on the eight-track, and that was when I dozed off. The next thing I knew, headlights were flashing in my rearview mirror. I steered to the side of the road, a tractor-trailer truck pulled up behind me, and a burly driver ran up to the window to let me know that he had watched my head roll back and forth until I fell asleep.

"You're lucky to be alive," he said. He warned me not

to drive anymore until I had gotten some rest—a warning I did not heed, because I had to be at work in the morning.

This was also the summer that Charlie Ed lost control of his drinking. One day he drove a forklift off the end of the loading dock, shattering a stack of drywall. I was ordered to clean up the mess. He was forbidden henceforth from operating machinery after lunch.

Many years later, reading Robert Hayden's poem "The Dogwood Trees," which celebrates an interracial friendship amid the hatred and violence provoked by the civil rights movement, I thought at once of my drunken afternoon with Charlie Ed.

THE DOGWOOD TREES

(for Robert Slagle)

Seeing dogwood trees in bloom,
I am reminded, Robin,
of our journey through the mountains
in an evil time.

Among rocks and rock-filled streams
white bracts of dogwood
clustered. Beyond, nearby, shrill slums
were burning,

the crooked crosses flared. We drove
with bitter knowledge
of the odds against comradeship we dared
and were at one.

The juxtaposition of rocks and delicate bracts of dogwood underscores Hayden's praise for the possibilities inherent in the yoking together of opposites—friendship, insight, political change. For those who dare to travel into the mountains, beyond the burning slums and crosses planted by the Klan, new vistas may appear, each promising pleasure, wisdom, or inspiration to travel farther yet into the unknown in search of—what? The imagination teems with ideas.

Hayden's use of the word *comradeship* invokes Walt Whitman's *Leaves of Grass*, the first edition of which was published in the tumultuous years leading up to the Civil War—another "evil time." Indeed the political divisions between the North and South fueled Whitman's poetic project, which proposed nothing less than the establishment of an equitable relationship between everyone and everything under the sun. "The known universe has one complete lover," he wrote, "and that is the greatest poet"—who was not Whitman, strictly speaking (though he had the highest regard for his own work), but the sum of poets through the ages. In a fragment recorded in his notebooks he declared, "I am the poet of slaves and of the masters of slaves / I am the poet of the body / And I am"—and then he drew a line down the page. This was his eureka moment, when he discovered the suitability of versets—a form adapted from Proverbs and the Psalms—to his aesthetic sensibility, and his book quickly took shape as he transformed into song love for his fellow man, sympathy for the things of the world, and the accumulating evidence of the flaw at the heart of the American experiment in liberty. Comradeship was Whitman's trope for healing the rift between human beings—which grew wider yet with the Confederate shelling of Fort Sumter.

His brother George enlisted on the Union side, in the Brooklyn Thirteenth Regiment, and during the next four years he fought in some of the most important battles of the war, including the Second Battle of Bull Run, Chantilly, Antietam, the Battle of the Wilderness, and Spotsylvania. When, in December 1862, at the end of the darkest year of the war, he was listed in the *New York Tribune* among the casualties from the Union defeat at Fredericksburg, Walt traveled to Washington to track him down. "It is hard to overstate the importance of George's war experiences on

Walt's career as a writer," David S. Reynolds argues in *Walt Whitman's America: A Cultural Biography*. "The war was at the very heart of his poetry, Walt would later say. But it was mainly because of George that Walt got close to the war." George's injury was slight—a facial wound from an exploding shell—but the sight of the war dead profoundly affected the poet, who wrote of one soldier, "Young man: I think this face of yours is the face of my dead Christ." He decided to stay in Washington to volunteer in the war hospitals, writing letters home for wounded soldiers—small acts of comradeship that fed the democratic current running through his work. "My book and the war are one," he wrote, "Merged into its spirit I and mine." He believed that war cleansed the land, at least temporarily, of some of its baser proclivities, and in his writings, in poetry and prose, it was his genius to summon his countrymen and -women to heed their better angels. The companionable precincts of his book remind us of what is noblest in American history: a spirit of comradeship such as what I experienced that afternoon in the lumberyard, sipping vodka straight with Charlie Ed.

An accident on the first weekend in August cut short my employment there. My parents and sisters had gone to the Outer Banks for vacation, and instead of joining them after work on Friday I drove to the Blue Ridge Mountains in southwestern Virginia for Stompin' 76, the so-called Woodstock of bluegrass music, which over three days would bring together the biggest names in old-time music: Doc Watson, Bonnie Raitt, Earl Scruggs, Lester Flatt, Ry Cooder, John Prine, Vassar Clements, the New Grass Revival, Papa John Creach, the Nitty Gritty Dirt Band. The traffic slowed to a stop north of Galax, so I parked on the side of the road, miles away from Doyle Lawson's farm, where more than one hundred thousand concertgoers were gathering, and joined the crowd walking toward the music. The road through the woods was packed with people my age or a little older, all white, many of them carrying sleeping bags and coolers, and the air was thick with the sweet smoke of pot. Helicopters whirred overhead, ferrying musicians to the stage. From time to time a motorcyclist wended through the crowd. I did not know a soul, no one knew where I was, and I took pleasure in being on my own, like a tree at the edge of a clearing. Maybe I would meet someone who would turn my life upside down?

Bartram's travels through the South furnished a template for literary naturalists, and it is tempting to view his determination to collect, identify, and name the varieties of flora and fauna he encountered as a means of keeping at bay the knowledge that his world was being overturned. He made no mention of the Revolutionary War in his book, which he did not complete until long after the last shot was fired, and yet it is present between the lines, in the same way that in the hundreds of poems Emily Dickinson wrote in 1862, when the Union seemed destined never to be made whole, she studiously avoided any reference to the carnage, which readers nevertheless hear in the back of their auditory imagination: "This is the Hour of Lead."

Not until the last moment did I register the sound of a motorcycle skidding on the pavement behind me. As I started to turn, the front wheel struck my leg, catapulting me headfirst into the bumper of a parked car, and then all went black. When I came to, strangers were hovering over me, blocking the sky; the motorcyclist was gone. An inventory of my injuries—concussion, sprained or broken wrist, throbbing hip—made me fear that my days as a midfielder were over, before it occurred to me that I might also be dying. Someone flagged down a van and told the driver to get me to the hospital as fast as possible—instructions he ignored, riding the brakes, refusing to honk the horn to clear the road. In the passenger seat was a scrawny man leaning out the window to hawk bags of pot and tabs of LSD, each sale requiring an elaborate negotiation. The van stopped and started, buyers came and went, and I was slipping in and out of consciousness, when we arrived at a clearing on a mountaintop. The dealer ordered me to get out, and the door was still open when the van sped away. I was led to a tent, where a policeman and a paramedic debated whether to transport me to the hospital in a helicopter or an ambulance. What they decided I do not recall, for the next thing I knew I was lying on a gurney in the corridor of an emergency room. On the next gurney was an unconscious man with a ponytail—an overdose victim, it seemed. A state trooper was jabbing him in the ribs.

"Wake up," he kept saying. "You're under arrest."

I thought he was talking to me, but before I could gather my wits to reply an orderly wheeled me into an examining room, where the nurse told me that X-rays were needed of my head, wrist, and hip. Some time passed before a doctor gave me a quick once-over, declining to order X-rays. My injuries were not life threatening, he said—though I would be in serious pain for weeks, thanks to a torn hip flexor that would mar the rest of my playing career. The doctor signed my release, warning me not to drive for at least twenty-four hours.

Out in the corridor the man on the gurney was still unconscious, handcuffed to the rail. The state trooper was nowhere to be seen. It took me hours to find my car, and then I could not raise my foot to shift gears. I had to use my sprained wrist to lift my injured thigh and set my foot down on the clutch, over and again. My head pounded the whole way home.

In Sickness and in Health

Dogwood anthracnose, a fungal infection, was first identified in *Cornus florida* in 1976. It arrived in the Pacific
Northwest on Asian dogwoods imported by nurserymen eager to sell trees that, unlike flowering dogwoods,
blossom after the leaves appear, creating a tapestry of
green and white that lasts into the summer. As *Cornus
kousa*, which is resistant to the fungus (tellingly named
Discula destructiva), took hold in yards from the suburbs
of Portland and Seattle to the Eastern Seaboard dogwood
anthracnose destroyed the native species on a massive
scale; within a decade of its discovery, nearly 80 percent
of the flowering dogwoods in Maryland's Catoctin Mountain Park, where Camp David is located, had died, leading President Ronald Reagan to complain to park officials
that something was wrong with the woods. The disease
spread into southern forests, and by 2010 mortality rates
were approaching 100 percent in parts of the Northeast

and the highlands of Appalachia. There is no remedy for the tan spots rimmed with purple that infect the leaves, forming cankers on twigs and branches and causing the bark to swell. Around Camp David, then, where American presidents have hosted political leaders since World War II, the flowering dogwoods are gone—a dying off that began around the time that Jimmy Carter brought together Egyptian president Anwar Sadat and Israeli prime minister Menachem Begin to negotiate the Camp David Accords.

Charles E. Little, who documented this natural catastrophe in *The Dying of the Trees*, a sobering look at forest decline caused by clear-cutting, acid rain, and disease, speculated that air pollution, climate change, and increased ultraviolet rays from the thinning ozone layer may explain the rapid spread of dogwood anthracnose. The loss for him was personal.

> With its graceful branches and luminous leaves, perfectly suited for a life under the overarching canopy of the oaks and hickories (or, sometimes, most beautifully, beneath the deep green tent of an old hemlock grove), the dogwood is a human-sized tree. It serves our needs in ways that the giants cannot, which is spiritual rather than practical. . . .

And so in modern times the tree became famous for its own sake. Now the function of the dogwood is to be found in its sheer beauty.

But it must be regarded in more than aesthetic terms. Because a single flowering dogwood can produce up to ten kilograms of high-protein berries in the fall, it is an invaluable source of food and cover for numerous species of birds and small game; its leaves are rich in calcium, nourishing animals and plants, and hasten the nutrient cycle, contributing to the overall health of the forest. "And no birds sing"—John Keats's line, which Rachel Carson used as an epigraph to *Silent Spring*, her environmental classic charting the harmful effects of pesticide use on birds—also applies to the declining songbird population. The silence in the woods is no longer the silence after music, but rather the silent grief that attends the death of a loved one.

This is a harbinger of things to come. Habitat destruction since World War II has greatly reduced the populations of songbirds such as the wood thrush, whip-poor-will, chipping sparrow, barn swallow, and scarlet tanager, not to mention all the colorful warblers— golden winged, black and white, and cerulean. A report from the National Audubon Society projects that by 2080 climate change will drive half of North America's approximately 650 bird species to live and breed in new, smaller places, with several dozen species likely headed for extinction, including the three-toed woodpecker, rufous hummingbird, and trumpeter swan. If it is true that birds are our early warning system, signaling everything from the change of seasons to levels of toxicity in our surroundings, then we must heed their silence now, in the same way that civilians in a besieged city regard the sudden departure of sentries from the watchtowers.

An Internet search of globalization's environmental impact yields millions of results, for the history of life on earth is the history of migration—of flora and fauna, people and goods, ideas and beliefs. Ships, planes, and automobiles crisscross the planet; information travels at the speed of light via optical fiber cables and orbiting satellites; seeds and diseases are borne aloft, begetting life and death. "Love makes the world go 'round," the singer croons, and as we spin through space, leaving our tracks in unlikely spots, there is no escaping the consequences of our travels. Thus an American nurseryman returns from a vacation in Asia with a cutting from a dogwood, *Cornus kousa*, which comes in Chinese, Japanese, and

Korean varieties. This he cultivates in his greenhouse, unaware that it carries anthracnose, which in the blink of an eye spreads through backyards and woodlands across America, wreaking havoc everywhere.

It happens that I played a role in destroying the native dogwood, working my way through graduate school in a nursery. After college, desperate to put as much distance as possible between my old life and whatever came next, I moved to Seattle to study creative writing at the University of Washington—though in the event much of my education took place at Munro's Nursery, where I shoveled mulch into pickup trucks, landscaped houses in the suburbs of Seattle, and extolled the virtues of *Cornus kousa* and other ornamental plants to customers, the majority of whom seemed oblivious to the fact that I knew nothing about what I was selling.

I started at the nursery in 1979, not long after the first article on anthracnose in the Pacific Northwest appeared in a trade newsletter. Plant pathologists at the Western Washington Research and Extension Center in Puyallup calculated that a significant percentage of the Pacific dogwood, *Cornus nuttallii*, was afflicted with the disease, which they did not think could be controlled with fungicides. Nor did their suggested remedies—pruning dead branches, raking up infected leaves—stem the outbreak, and so within a year native dogwoods were dying as far away as New York and Connecticut. If Jerry Munro, the owner of the nursery, read the article (and he probably did, keen as he was for information that might help his business), he never mentioned anthracnose in my hearing—which was unsurprising. My knowledge of botany was rudimentary; much of the wisdom he dispensed in my first months on the job (and some of his instructions) fell on deaf ears. A friend joked that I worked with plants because they had no moving parts, though in truth I had little more than a basic appreciation of their beauty. It is a wonder that Jerry did not fire me.

He was more forgiving than his competitors might have thought, his entrepreneurial spirit tempered by an innate sense of right and wrong. Born on Christmas Eve in 1916, in Bismarck, North Dakota, he moved with his family to Seattle when he was eleven and went into business for himself selling flowers from his mother's garden on Queen Anne Hill. During the Depression, he acquired a professional photography license to document botanical trips up the Fraser River in Canada, and he studied horticulture at Washington State University. There he met his wife, Jean, and with their first child on the way, he gave up a graduate fellowship at the University of Washington to work at Boeing. After the war he opened a nursery, which in a series of locations would supply plants and trees to gardeners all around Puget Sound. The final incarnation of Munro's was on his property in Kenmore, which, according to a photograph on his website, featured "the biggest native dogwood in King County, over 80 feet tall and 40 feet wide." Jerry passed away in the summer of 2014, at the age of ninety-eight. He spent his last morning working in the nursery.

He was a small, wiry man, a champion wrestler in high school and college who late in life fought a burglar to the ground. Every day, in good weather and bad, he wore rubber boots and the same unbuttoned plaid shirt to the nursery, where he was always the last to leave. He had a mischievous streak, and soon I was collecting stories about him: how as a graduate student he came home from a hunting trip with a jammed twelve-gauge shotgun, which he tried to clear by tapping on the floor. The gun went off, blowing a hole through the ceiling of the apartment below, scattering pellets in the food of the family eating dinner. They were not amused.

One day Jerry went into the woods to dig up maidenhair ferns to use for landscaping, though at the time they were on the protected list, and there he came upon a patch of tall pot plants. The sight so enraged him that he pulled the plants up by the roots, threw them into the back of his covered pickup, and drove into town, intending to turn them over to the authorities. But on his way to the police station he decided to stop for lunch at a hotel on the main street, parking right in front. After polishing off a hamburger and a cup of coffee, he fell asleep at the table—only to be awakened by a policeman, who had spotted the contraband in his truck.

Another morning, after a rare snowstorm, a detective drove into the nursery in a van loaded with plastic bags of sterilized dirt, which had been confiscated from an indoor pot operation. What tipped off the police flying over the area in a helicopter to survey the damage from the storm was the sight of one barn with no snow on its roof, thanks to the heat from its grow lights. The detective offered the dirt for fifty cents a bag, which we sold an hour later, for ten times that amount, to a bedraggled hippie in dark glasses. Jerry wrote down his license-plate number, called the detective, and within a week the unopened bags of dirt were ours to sell again.

Then there was the day Jerry drove into the nursery parking lot and, seeing a creditor waiting for him with a sheaf of bills in hand, circled the parking lot, smiling, and kept driving. The creditor chased him to the road, where he threw the papers at Jerry's pickup and then instructed me to collect them, unless I wished to see my boss in jail. This was no idle threat. Jerry's frugality, which he traced to his Scottish heritage, translated into a chronic inability to pay his bills—and into brushes with the law. One experiment ended badly when he stopped paying his bookkeeper, who went to the labor board to disclose irregularities in Jerry's accounting practices. Among other things, it turned out that new deductions from our paychecks—minuscule amounts like $2.18 or $1.79—did not go into a pension plan, as Jerry had led us to believe, but into his own pocket.

"It's Jerry's pension plan," the foreman joked.

After everyone had gone home one Friday except Jerry and me, two policemen arrived to arrest him for some financial misdeed. Before they led him off in handcuffs, he ordered me to wait for his call. It was hours in coming. To pay his bail, he told me, I was to take $250 from the till—which had but $80 in it. Add your pay, Jerry said. I reminded him that he had not paid me what I was owed. Then call Jean, he said, growing agitated. His wife, who was also short on cash, thought it would not hurt him to spend a night in jail, so I left a message with the police that we would bail him out the next day, as soon as we had taken in enough money.

The nursery was busy on Saturday morning, and we could have sprung him by lunch, if we had so desired. But the foreman preferred to wait until the close of business—"It's pleasant not having him around," he said—by which time Jerry was in a cool rage. He came straight to the nursery and counted the money in the till, rejecting out of hand the foreman's explanation that we had been too busy to get away.

He could not bear to let anything go to waste—time or plants. The greenhouse was stocked with orchids collected on his trips to Hawai'i, where the local practice of discarding them once they had finished blooming offended his sensibilities. At Munro's, sick or dying trees, including native and imported dogwoods, were replanted in an overgrown area, fertilized, and then forgotten by everyone but Jerry.

"They'll come back," he would say, a twinkle in his eye.

Some trees restored to health I would ball and burlap for transplanting to a client's yard—a task I loved. First I cleared the weeds from around the base of the tree, and then I dug a trench a foot or so from the trunk, carving a root ball in the shape of a large pumpkin. Angling my spade into the earth, I cut the roots, rocking the ball until it could be lifted free. This I wrapped in burlap and pinned together with oval-headed nails, like a diaper. Sometimes Jerry sent me into the woods to dig trees, and once to a nursery near Everett, where I worked for a week to root-ball azaleas and rhododendrons. The pleasure I took in preparing plants for transplanting would remain inexplicable to me until I reached late middle age, when I realized that in the course of moving from place to place, from Seattle to Salt Lake City, Santa Fe, New Orleans, Portland, New England, and Iowa, transplanting had become the story of my life.

It could have turned out much differently.

At the end of my first summer in Seattle, a friend arranged a freelance technical writing job for me, which paid $75 an hour—more than ten times what I was making at the nursery. A start-up software company sent an incomprehensible text about a computer operating system, the editing of which bored me to tears. My friend's tip that the company was hiring did not interest me in the least. For all I know the position I did not even bother to apply for was at Microsoft, where I might have earned millions of dollars. But in those days I preferred to devote myself to poetry and plants. The information age was upon us, and before long technological innovations would make possible the instantaneous transmission of ideas around the world. I was content to read poems and root-ball Asian dogwoods, which produce fruit too big for birds to digest.

"The Dream of the Rood"

To satisfy the language requirement for my graduate degree, I studied Old English for a year, in a class divided between linguists, who took careful notes on index cards, and poets, who were mainly interested in the music of our origins. Old English vocabulary and grammar have receded from my memory, but I retain a vivid sense of the hemistich at the heart of its poetry, the heavily alliterative verse line rediscovered in our time by Ezra Pound and W. H. Auden, Richard Wilbur and W. S. Merwin: "Bitter breast-cares have I abided, / Known on my keel many a care's hold," as Pound wrote in "The Seafarer." This music still echoes in our language, which has undergone such radical changes in the last millennium as to be unrecognizable to the bards who performed their poems in the mead hall to the accompaniment of a harp. They entertained the royal court and its warriors, preserving the history and oral traditions of the Germanic peoples associated with the Anglo-Saxon settlement of Britain—a process of invasion and acculturation that began in the fifth century and ended with the Norman Conquest in 1066, giving shape to the spirit and culture of the island. For my literary apprenticeship I went to the source of English poetry, translating *Beowulf* in its entirety at the rate of a hundred lines a night, as well as bawdy riddles, heroic tales, and religious poems, including "The Dream of the Rood," the most beautiful work of Anglo-Saxon literature.

This first dream-vision poem in English was probably composed in the eighth century. (Runic inscriptions of eighteen verses appear on the Ruthwell Cross in Northumbria, an eighteen-foot-tall stone cross, which was raised sometime after the local population converted to Christianity in 660, destroyed by Protestant iconoclasts in 1642, and then patiently reassembled two centuries later by a Scottish divine.) But the full text of "The Dream of the Rood" did not come to light until 1822, when a parchment manuscript of homilies and poems was discovered in the library of the Vercelli Cathedral near Milan; how the Vercelli Book, one of four surviving Old English poetic codices, got to Italy is unknown. It easily could have vanished.

The poem opens with a warrior recounting his dream

of a tree towering in the sky, suffused with a golden light and gleaming with jewels—the "tree of victory" on which Christ was crucified. Bands of angels look on as the guilt-ridden narrator, stained with sin, watches "the lively beacon" change, now covered with blood and gore, now "bedecked with treasure." This image calls to mind the vision vouchsafed to Constantine I in 312, before the Battle of the Milvian Bridge over the Tiber River north of Rome, of a cross in the sky bearing the message "With this sign, you will conquer." Constantine ordered his soldiers to paint a symbol of the Crucifixion on their shields, merging the first two letters of Christ's name in Greek—☧—and then they marched to victory over the army of his rival emperor, Maxentius, who in the course of battle drowned in the Tiber. Thus began the Christianization of the Roman Empire. Constantine called the first ecumenical council in Nicaea in 325; five years later, he consecrated a second imperial capital, Constantinople, on the site of the ancient Greek colony of Byzantium. Constantinople became the center of power after the sack of Rome in 410, and in 596, Pope Gregory the Great, who had served as papal ambassador to Constantinople, sent missionaries to Britain to convert the Anglo-Saxons. The originality of "The Dream of the Rood" depends in part on its use of heroic language to explore a religious theme, creating tension between two worldviews—pagan and Christian, war and faith. The relationship between dream and reality is mirrored in the clash between two ways of being, one laid on top of another, like the two beams of the cross: a palimpsest subject to endless interpretation.

Anything can happen in a dream, and so the tree begins to speak, describing for the warrior how it was cut down in a copse, moved from its roots by "strong enemies," and propped on a hill, where it sees "the Lord of all mankind / Hasten with eager zeal that He might mount / Upon me." The Argentinian writer Jorge Luis Borges noted in a lecture on Anglo-Saxon poetry that "the cross trembles when it feels Christ's embrace. It is as if the cross were Christ's woman, his wife; the cross shares the pain of the crucified God." It is made wet by the Savior's blood, bears the scars of the nails pounded into its limbs to secure him—"the wounds of open malice," in the poet's words—and grieves when he dies. The corpse cools, the cross is cut down and buried with it, and then servants of the Lord dig up the cross to decorate it with gold and silver. The warrior is ordered to tell its story, a prototype of the modern literary tradition of giving voice to the things of the earth, a defining feature of the best nature writing.

From Rainer Maria Rilke, Francis Ponge, and Pablo Neruda to Aldo Leopold and Rachel Carson, poets and writers have adopted nonhuman perspectives to portray Creation in all its wonder and possibility, illuminating new means of understanding the human condition and our place in the great chain of being. "Declare in words this is the tree of glory," the cross commands, "On which Almighty God once suffered torments / For mankind's many sins, and for the deeds / Of Adam long ago." Salvation will come to those who believe in it.

In my imagination that tree has always been a dogwood. From my first reading of the poem, in Richard Hamer's translation, through my own attempts to render it in English, I had in mind the ridged bark and white blossoms of the dogwood above my childhood fort. For I served my literary apprenticeship under the sign of the dogwood, the Tree of Life in the Sky World of the Mohawks and the cross of Christian tradition. And I was drawn to the martial imagery of "The Dream of the Rood," which presents Christ not as a passive sufferer but as the leader of a successful expedition to the Kingdom of God. The narrator wishes to honor "the tree of triumph" so that he, too, may join the "multitude of spirits" flanking the Son of Man in the divine war for the human heart. The poem concludes, "The Ruler entered into His own land." In this cosmology, where everything has sacred value, war and faith are entwined at the root.

It is no accident that the poem took shape as pagan culture was giving way to Christianity: civilizational clashes have inspired artistic expression from time immemorial, as people seek to make sense of their new circumstances. War is frequently the catalyst for change, and "The Dream of the Rood" marks this change in a dramatic fashion, the pagan-warrior ethos bleeding through the religious message, revealing the contours of a vanished world. Some have noted that in blank verse, iambic pentameter, the dominant line of English poetry from the time of Chaucer until the last century, one may count four strong stresses instead of five, the ghost of Anglo-Saxon meter lurking in the background, like music heard from a distance. One story gives way to another, and in the new dispensation traces of the past endure.

The Greenhouse

"What was the greenhouse?" Theodore Roethke asks in a notebook entry, reflecting on his father's nursery in Saginaw, Michigan. "It was a jungle, and it was paradise; it was order and disorder: Was it an escape? No, for it was a reality harsher than reality." It was also a "symbol for the whole of life," according to the poet, "a womb, a heaven-on-earth." His memories of the nursery provided him with material for *The Lost Son and Other Poems* (1948), the book that announced his arrival as a poet to be reckoned with. "Sticks-in-a-drowse droop over sugary loam," he writes in "Cuttings," the opening poem, which celebrates the propagation of cut stems as a metaphor for the growth of the poet's mind, an urgent theme for literary apprentices since at least the time that William Wordsworth composed the first version of *Prelude* in 1805. Roethke ranks "this urge, wrestle, resurrection of dry sticks" above the saint's quest for eternal life, an easier task in his view than "lopped limbs" putting down new roots; what he felt in his veins and bones, "the small waters seeping upward, / the tight grains parting at last," I dreamed of in the greenhouse at Munro's.

Some of Roethke's students at the University of Washington went on to become significant poets, including Richard Hugo, Carolyn Kizer, David Wagoner, and James Wright, and his tutelary spirit still reigned in the creative writing program when I enrolled. Wagoner would invoke his teachings in our poetry workshop to explain how rhythm can serve to reinforce or counter meaning and to discuss ways of courting inspiration, the necessity of accurate description, and other intricacies of the art. He had assembled from Roethke's notebooks, from "fragments of poetry, aphorisms, jokes, memos, journal entries, random phrases, bits of dialogue, literary and philosophical commentary, rough drafts of whole poems, quotations, etc.," a magnetic book, *Straw for the Fire*, learning in the process how the poet worked:

> Roethke apparently let his mind rove freely, moment
> by moment in the early stages of composition, from the
> practical to the transcendental, from the lame and halting
> to the beautiful, from the comic to the terrible, from the

literal to the surreal, seizing whatever he might from the language, but mulling over and taking soundings of every syllable.

This version of automatic writing, which led Roethke to discover his own subject, style, and voice in his break-through book, *The Lost Son and Other Poems*, I adopted as a method of composition. What surprised me was how often dogwoods surfaced in my early drafts of poems. It was Roethke's friend Stanley Kunitz who argued that "at the center of every poetic imagination is a cluster of key images that go back to the poet's childhood and that are usually associated with pivotal experiences, not necessarily traumatic. Poets are always revisiting the state of their innocence, as if to be renewed by it." If Roethke's journey to his childhood yielded poems about carnations, trans-planting, and three old women who worked for his father, "plot[ing] for more than themselves," I found a tree, a fort, and a house swept out to sea in a hurricane—images integral to the structure of my imagination, which I was learning to explore in poetry workshops and the nursery.

In his essay "The Wisdom of the Body," Kunitz sketched out an alternative approach to a literary apprenticeship, which depended upon broadening one's perspective:

When I am asked by young poets what advice I have to offer them about the conduct of their lives, I am inclined to warn them about the dangers of hothouse anemia. "Do something else," I tell them, "develop any other skill, turn to any other branch of knowledge. Learn how to use your hands. Try woodworking, birdwatching, gardening, sailing, weaving, pottery, archaeology, oceanography, spelunking, animal husbandry—take your pick. Whatever activity you engage in, as trade or hobby or field study, will tone up your body and clear your head. At the very least it will help you with your metaphors."

Poets should be generalists, not specialists, Kunitz continued, which made sense to me, and his warnings about "hothouse anemia" I took to heart, attempting to balance what I was hearing in my classes with my experiences in the nursery. His beliefs may have stemmed from witnessing Roethke's battles with mental illness, which periodically landed him in the psychiatric ward. (One day he told his students they looked like cattle, climbed onto the window ledge of the second-story classroom, and stood there until a fireman coaxed him back inside.) According to Kunitz, Roethke "could brag of belonging to the brotherhood of mad poets that includes William

Blake, John Clare, and Christopher Smart, with each of whom he was able to identify himself as 'lost.'" Yet in his notebooks he also admonished himself to work with his hands as a means of dealing with his manic depression. I followed this advice to the letter, for in the nursery I discovered that manual labor could alleviate my anxiety about the difficulties—artistic, financial, and spiritual—of pursuing a literary vocation. The physical exhaustion that came over me on the way home from work was a balm for my soul.

Roethke was just fifty-five years old when he died of a heart attack while swimming in a friend's pool on Bainbridge Island. (The pool was later filled in and converted into a Zen garden.) His last book, *The Far Field*, published posthumously in 1964, opens with a North American sequence of meditations, featuring Whitmanesque catalogues of imagery from the natural world—tides rippling over "low, barnacled, elephant-colored rocks," kingfishers and eagles in flight, the silence made by the light. Illumination is the theme, the stages of which are recounted in lines of varying lengths. "In the long journey out of the self," he writes, "There are many detours, washed-out interrupted raw places" in the search for "the moment of turning"; the confrontation with mortality is essential to the experience of awe, which may occur on a desolate stretch of road, on a spit of land by the Pacific, or in the wilderness of memory. Spiritual regeneration is what the poet earns from attending to the world around him and the motions of his mind.

"The Rose," the final poem in the sequence, begins, "There are those to whom place is unimportant, / But this place, where sea and fresh water meet, / Is important." Roethke travels to the edge of the continent to ask, "What do they tell us, sound and silence?" He registers birdsong, the cries of towhee and owl, and then the silence in which he sways outside himself, his eye lighting on a wild rose flowering "in its true place," in the sea wind, among the morning glories in a briary hedge, where the creek winds down to the shore. This prompts a memory:

And I think of roses, roses,
White and red, in the wide six-hundred-foot
      greenhouses,
And my father standing astride the cement benches,
Lifting me high over the four-foot stems, the Mrs.
      Russells, and his own elaborate hybrids,
And how those flowerheads seemed to flow toward
      me, to beckon me, only a child, out of myself.

What need for heaven, then,
With that man, and those roses?

The recollection of an ecstatic moment from childhood rouses the adult poet to devise an escape route from
the prison of the self, a secular means of transcendence
born of close attention to worlds within and without—the
same things that beckoned me to explore.

Metaphors

The dogwood, then, as metaphor—of the march of civilization, the Passion, growth and decline, love and war. Call it a form of knowledge, a way of illumination, an expression of nature's variety. It is part of the Tree of Life, which in different cultures may represent fertility, immortality, purity, the link between heaven and earth, or the interconnection of all things. In *The Origin of Species*, Charles Darwin uses this figure to describe evolution:

> From the first growth of the tree, many a limb and branch
> has decayed and dropped off; and these fallen branches of
> various sizes may represent those whole orders, families,
> and genera which have now no living representatives, and
> which are known to us only in a fossil state. As we here
> and there see a thin, straggling branch springing from
> a fork low down in a tree, and which by some chance
> has been favoured and is still alive on its summit, so we

occasionally see an animal like the Ornithorhynchus [platypus] or Lepidosiren [South American lungfish], which in some small degree connects by its affinities two large branches of life, and which has apparently been saved from fatal competition by having inhabited a protected station. As buds give rise by growth to fresh buds, and these, if vigorous, branch out and overtop on all sides many a feebler branch, so by generation I believe it has been with the great Tree of Life, which fills with its dead and broken branches the crust of the earth, and covers the surface with its ever-branching and beautiful ramifications.

Paleontology, a burgeoning field of inquiry in the nineteenth century, inspired Darwin and others to examine the relationship between living and extinct organisms: how the dead and broken branches of the Tree of Life, preserved in the fossil record, revealed the "beautiful ramifications" of evolution, which radically altered our sense of things. Take the diversity of dogwood species descending, presumably, from a common ancestor. In their authoritative book on all things *Cornus*, Paul Cappiello and Don Shadow inventory scores of hybrids, some naturally occurring and some bred by nurserymen, whose names might bring to mind the catalogue of ships in *The Iliad*. Homer lists in a passage of 275 lines the captains and cities of the Greeks who sailed to Troy, rehearsing their names and genealogies in a celebration of the forces assembled to retrieve Helen, the wife of Agamemnon, whose quarrel with Achilles inspires the action of the epic poem. A friend used to read this passage aloud to her daughter at bedtime, lulling her to sleep. One might praise nature through a recitation of the distinctive names bestowed on the shrubs and trees of the *Cornus* family: Bunchberry and Bear Berry, Kinnikinnick and Downeaster, Rough- and Round-Leaved, Silky and Tatarian, Big Leaf and Grey, Bloodtwig and Midwinter Fire, Siberian Pearls and Snakeroot, Black-Fruited and Red-Stemmed, Cardinal and Cheyenne, Garden Glow and Isanti, Silver and Gold and Sunshine, Pagoda and Giant Dogwood, Wedding Cake Tree and June Snow, Ragdoll and American Beauty, Angel Wings and Appalachian Spring, Ascending and Autumn Gold, Big Bouquet and Blonde Luster, Big Girl and Bonnie, Cherokee Princess and Cloud Nine, Daybreak and First Lady, Fragrant Cloud and Geronimo, Gold Braid and Green Glow, Imperial White and Juanita, Moonglow and Mystery, Ozark Spring and Pendula, Pink Sachet and Prairie Snow, President Ford and Pygmy, Rainbow and Red Giant, September Dog and Sterling Silver, Weaver's White and White Love, World's Fair and First Choice, Avalanche and Baby Splash, Bonfire and China Girl, Claudia and Doubloon, Fanfare and Fireworks, Marble and Milky Way, Miss Petty and Par Four, Pendula and Prolific, Southern Cross and Square Dance, Steeple and Sunsplash, Trinity Star and Triple Crown, Waterfall and Wolf Eyes, North Star and Pilgrim . . .

Eye of the Hurricane

"After all, I don't know why I am always asking for private, individual, selfish miracles," wrote Anne Morrow Lindbergh, "when every year there are miracles like white dogwood." This was what I felt, more or less, lying beside a dark-haired woman at daybreak, under a blossoming dogwood at the university. After a party at Gas Works Park, we had walked through the night, from Lake Union to Fremont to Wallingford, talking about this and that until we came to the fountain on the south side of campus, where she suggested that we find someplace to lie down. Now as the light gathered in the branches above us I marveled at my good fortune, pushing away the nagging worry that her heart would never be mine. We had known each other for the better part of a year, during which she had betrayed no sign of interest in me, and it was only now, when she was about to leave for a summer job in Maine, that something seemed to change. A current of feeling was running between us when I boarded the bus to the nursery, where I worked through the morning with uncommon energy, shoveling bark into pickups, loading plants into cars, dispensing erroneous information to customers. But the lack of sleep caught up with me at lunch, and as the day wore on I realized it would take a miracle to win her over.

That spring I was doing an independent study on the novels of John Fowles with a writing professor who, I suspected, had not read the Englishman in some time, if at all. Which left me free to interpret in my own fashion scenes from *The Collector*, *The Magus*, *The French Lieutenant's Woman*, and *Daniel Martin*. To figure out the method of Fowles's magic, I committed to memory some of his sentences and even a paragraph or two, borrowed characters for a short story I was writing, imitated his style in the pastiche I turned in for my final paper—which I knew the professor would not read. But the key to his fiction, Fowles divulged in *The Tree*, a book-length essay published in 1979, not long before I went to work at the nursery, was to be found in his relationship to nature, specifically to trees. He took a dim view of the care with which his father tended the prize-winning apple and pear trees in his garden, pruning them in an orderly manner alien to Fowles's own more unruly sensibility. What the novelist craved—"space, wildness, hills, woods"—lay beyond the confines of his father's garden; his "orchards" were woods and deserted copses in the west of England and France. His passion for natural history and the countryside led him to conclude that in its devotion to the scientific method humankind had ignored at its peril the complexity of experience, mistaking the narrow frame of analysis for the meaning of life:

> Ordinary experience, from waking second to second, is in fact highly synthetic (in the sense of combinative or constructive), and made of a complexity of strands, past memories and present perceptions, times and places, private and public history, hopelessly beyond science's powers to analyse. It is quintessentially "wild," in the sense my father disliked so much: unphilosophical, irrational, uncontrollable, incalculable. In fact it corresponds very closely—despite our endless efforts to "garden," to invent disciplining social and intellectual systems—with wild nature. Almost all the richness of our personal existence derives from this synthetic and eternally present "confused" consciousness of both internal and external reality, and not least because we know it is beyond the analytical, or destructive, capacity of science.

Fowles translated his faith in nature into aesthetic doctrine. "I have always loathed flat and treeless country," he wrote. "Time there seems to dominate, it ticks remorselessly like a clock. But trees warp time, or rather create a variety of times: here dense and abrupt, there calm and sinuous—never plodding, mechanical, inescapably monotonous." An expanded sense of time is thus integral to his fiction, notably in the metahistorical voice and multiple endings of *The French Lieutenant's Woman*, and in the metaphysical questions posed in *Daniel Martin*, a coming-of-age story set by turns in rural England, Hollywood and the American Southwest, Oxford and London, and on a tour of Egypt, Lebanon, and Syria. When a playwright-turned-screenwriter is called home from Hollywood to see a dying friend, he embarks on a journey of self-discovery, told in first and third person, exploring his past, confronting himself and the consequences of decisions he made long ago, attempting to come to terms with what he has lost along the way—the only woman he ever truly loved, his estranged daughter, his art, his identity.

The novel opens with the teenaged protagonist harvesting wheat in the English countryside with four older men and a pair of draft horses. He carries sheaves to stooks, "a stook being four pairs of sheaves and a single 'to close the door' at each end," until they stop for lunch. Under an ash tree, they eat thick slices of ham and bread smothered in butter, washed down with cider from tin mugs. August 1942. From the distance comes the wail of a siren. The boy scans the blue sky: nothing. Then the thump of artillery from a wing cannon, three seconds of silence, another thump. The sky is still empty, until a German plane suddenly appears two hundred feet overhead, "violent machinery at full stretch, screaming in an agony of vicious fear." The boy knows he is about to die. Both horses rear, one canters away, and the plane flies by, "trailing its savage roar." Two men run after the horse, which stops at the edge of the uncut wheat, and soon the work resumes. The reaper is almost finished with the field when a crowd gathers for another harvest. Rabbits are flushed from the last swathes of wheat, chased by a gypsy's lurcher or pounced upon and flailed with sticks by old men and boys: a massacre inspired by the devil, Fowles writes, who "honors fields at cutting time." Later the boy will return to the scene of the crime to carve his initials and the date on a beech tree: "Deep incisions in the bark, peeling the gray skin away to the sappy green of the living stem. Adieu, my boyhood and my dream."

Thus begins a bildungsroman in the form of a guide

to consciousness, which for the writer is rooted in place. And the theme is time, in all its twists and turns: the changes it brings, the losses it incurs. Who does not want to escape the tyranny of time, which may dissolve in lovemaking, ecstatic experience, awe? Past, present, and future merge for artists in the act of creation, when their preparation, materials, and labor come together, illuminating some part of their experience. Fowles explores this phenomenon in his novel, altering the chronology of events and switching points of view, presenting time as not a linear process but a circular construct, in which the present contains both the past and the future, just as a tree contains in its leaves and branches the memory of its seeding and the promise of its inevitable decline and fall.

The epigraph to *Daniel Martin* is from Antonio Gramsci's *Prison Notebooks*: "The crisis consists precisely in the fact that the old is dying and the new cannot be born; in this interregnum a great variety of morbid symptoms appears." Though I did not grasp its significance at the time, I was coming of age during the information-technology revolution, which hastened the end of the Cold War. In due course I would record some of the morbid symptoms that appeared in the former Yugoslavia, whose wars of succession were described by a Bosnian friend not as a clash between urban and rural dwellers, as policy analysts and journalists routinely defined it, but as one between those who used computers and those who did not. I was slow to adopt the new technology—my Luddite instincts were strong—and in the interregnum between the order in which I was born and raised and what was being devised by software designers working nearby I tried to document on a manual typewriter what I saw and experienced, recalled and imagined.

The key to my writing, I learned that year, was also to be found in my relationship to nature, specifically the wooded hills of Brookside and the dunes on the south shore of Long Island, where my father's side of the family had summered since the 1930s. The house in Quogue was built across from the drawbridge over Shinnecock Inlet, and our days were marked by the sound of waves crashing onshore, the cry of seagulls, the tolling of the bell when the bridge was raised to let a sailboat through. In one of my earliest memories my father is teaching me to fly a kite in high winds. It is overcast; the surf is too rough for swimming; no one else is on the beach. I am happy to escape the air of menace hanging over our house, where my mother is packing; we are leaving because of the barometer on the wall, which she keeps checking. The kite darts this way and that, spiraling upward, and when my father hands me the reel my glee is boundless. Tugged by the wind, I let out more line, wondering what will happen if I reach the end. Will I be lifted off my feet? But then the wind dies, and the kite plummets into the dunes. My father takes the reel from me, an eerie silence growing around us. *This is the eye of the hurricane,* he explains, winding in the tangled line. I look up, expecting to see a giant pupil; the ray of sunlight funneling through the clouds dazzles me. *Time to go,* he says.

When our house was swept out to sea, everything vanished except my bedroom. (Decades later, during a panel discussion on writing and the environment, a friend said that indigenous elders might interpret this fact to mean that I was destined to witness a great deal of chaos from the safety of my bedroom, to which another friend replied, "A great deal of chaos in his bedroom!") The house was rebuilt behind the dunes, and for seven summers I played in the sand, bodysurfed, fished in the inlet, and sailed around an island consisting of a house that surging waves had pushed into Shinnecock Bay, mindful at every change in the weather that it could all be taken away—as indeed it was when the house was sold after my grandfather died.

As for the woman who lay with me at daybreak under a blossoming dogwood? She moved to Maine later in the spring, and I never saw her again.

Still Life

A customer was waiting impatiently for the nursery to open when I arrived one Sunday morning. He knew what he wanted—dozens of bunchberry dogwoods (*Cornus canadensis*), a ground cover found in boreal forests in the northern tier of the United States and Canada that happens to be the fastest-moving plant on earth, its white flowers blooming in less than half a millisecond, a four-petal explosion that eclipses the snap of the Venus flytrap. Its stamens catapult grains of pollen at a speed of nearly ten feet per second—2,400 times the acceleration of gravity and 800 times the force that astronauts experience during liftoff, according to researchers at Williams College, who documented the flowers opening on video shot at one thousand to ten thousand frames per second. They speculate that bunchberries require such propulsion to spread their pollen on the wind and the bees and other insects that trigger this phenomenon—which it shares with its sister species, the Swedish cornel (*Cornus suecica*), growing in Europe and Asia as well as Alaska, Greenland, and Labrador. What a marvelous thing: a carpet of bunchberries blossoming in the woods from May until July—a picture of perfect repose, white four-petal-like bracts containing thousands of flowers per square meter—is a site of pure speed. The customer and I loaded the dwarf dogwoods into his truck, and when we went into the greenhouse to ring up the sale he produced a newspaper advertisement, which in my haste to conclude the transaction I misread, charging him considerably less than what the plants were supposed to sell for. It was not until he drove away that the gravity of my mistake became clear: I had cost the nursery more than two hundred dollars.

"Waste makes haste. I hurry to the dump," the poet Mark Strand wrote, reversing the idiom about the hazards of acting too quickly. My carelessness might have cost me my job.

Presently the foreman arrived. When I told him what I had done, he removed a tin of Skoal from his hip pocket, placed a pinch on his lower lip, stared at me. "Uh-oh, Gunga Din," he said—and then he devised a plan: to move boxwoods from the back of the nursery into the space formerly occupied by the bunchberries, hoping our eagle-eyed boss would not notice. For the rest of the day I held my breath whenever Jerry escorted a customer by the boxwoods. Once he even stopped to look at the new arrangement, less in admiration than in bewilderment, or so it seemed to me. But he said nothing, not then or in the coming days, and by the next weekend I had convinced myself that the danger was past.

During a lull on Sunday afternoon, when I was leaning on my shovel by the mound of bark, Jerry motioned for me to get into his pickup.

"Where are we going?" I asked.

"You'll see," he said.

Ordinarily garrulous, he drove in silence toward Lake Washington, refusing to answer my questions—which acquired a touch of desperation as we approached the floating bridge. The sun was high, and it seemed to take forever to cross the lake; by the time we reached the causeway through the marshlands of the arboretum in Seattle I had concluded that Jerry was going to fire me, albeit in an unusual manner. Why would he drive me home? I wondered, sinking into my seat, resigned to enjoying my remaining minutes of employment. But then he passed my exit and turned north onto the interstate, heading toward Canada. Mile after mile passed in silence. I thought perhaps he

was so angry about the bunchberries that he was planning to leave me at the border, when he took the exit to
Everett and pulled into the parking lot of a shopping mall.
From his wallet he removed three twenty-dollar bills—
about what I was owed, minus the cost of the plants—and
smiled. I wondered how long it would take to hitchhike to
Seattle.

"I need you to do something for me," he said.

In the mall there was an exhibit of paintings by local
artists, including his wife, Jean, who had, to her chagrin,
failed to attract any buyers. Jerry wanted me to wander
through the exhibit like a connoisseur (in my muddy
boots, jeans, and work shirt) before circling back to Jean's
work, pretending to fall in love with it. I was to ask the
woman handling sales to tell me about this gifted artist,
praising her originality, and then I was to buy one of her
cheaper paintings, extolling its virtues to the saleswoman
as knowledgeably as I could.

I bounded into the mall, relieved to still have a job.
The exhibit occupied the hall between two rows of stores,
and since I was on the clock I took my time looking over
the oil paintings and watercolors, all of a pedestrian qual-
ity. The still life I bought, an impressionistic rendering of
flowers in a vase, reminded me of paintings my grand-

mother made, a number of which had been swept out to sea in the hurricane. The saleswoman politely answered my questions, wrote out a receipt, and said the artist would be pleased to know her painting was in good hands.

Jerry was quite talkative on the drive back to Kirkland, pointing out native trees and shrubs along the road—vine maple and cascara, salal and bearberry—and instructing me at considerable length in the Japanese art of bonsai: the wiring and clamping and pruning of woody plants selected for their beauty and hardiness; the patience required to train the branches to grow in new directions; the elegant shapes that might appeal to his customers. It was closing time when we arrived at the nursery. He presented the painting to the foreman and left.

"Gunga Din," the foreman said, "Jerry's full of surprises."

But the story did not end there. Jean came to the nursery one day the next week, a rare occurrence, and strode up to me.

"You think you're pretty clever," she said.

"What do you mean?" I asked innocently.

"Jerry's so stupid," she said. "I found the receipt for my painting in his pants."

Compost

The dump truck parked in the back of the nursery was filled with flattened five-gallon cans, plastic trays, pesticide containers, newspapers, food wrappings. What could not be composted wound up in the truck, which I did not know even ran until one rainy autumn morning when Jerry told me to climb into the passenger's seat. We set out for a landscaping job in Issaquah. He was silent the whole trip, once again refusing to answer my questions, intent, it seemed, on the slick road. Nor would he explain why he turned down a muddy driveway a mile and a half short of the work site. He pulled up in front of a ranch house belonging to a creditor, backed onto the lawn, and raised the bed to dump ten tons of trash on the grass.

"What are you *doing*?" I asked, appalled.

Jerry shook his head, a devilish grin spreading across his face, and shifted into first gear to drive away, only to become stuck in the mud. He revved the engine, rocking forward and back, and as the tires churned, sinking into the earth, his smirk gave way to a look of panic. He switched off the engine and ordered me to go get the foreman. As I started up the driveway, he cried, "Run!" But my boots were heavy, the mud was deep, and so I jogged to the road before slowing to a walk. When I got to the work site, the foreman was waiting in his car. He was neither surprised to hear what Jerry had done nor sympathetic to his plight. He shook his head. Smiled.

"Have some coffee," he said, passing me the thermos. He took a dip of snuff and refilled his cup. Ten more minutes went by before we set out to rescue Jerry.

In those days I was reading Walt Whitman's post–Civil War poems, which reveal how the carnage darkened his understanding of the human condition, and at the sight of the debris scattered across the lawn I recalled "This Compost," a poem that enacts a journey from terror to acceptance of the complicated processes at the heart of existence. Whitman, startled by something when he thinks he is "safest," retreats from the woods he loves and poses a series of difficult questions:

O how can it be that the ground itself does not sicken?
How can you be alive you growths of spring?

How can you furnish health you blood of herbs, roots,
    orchards, grain?

Are they not continually putting distemper'd corpses
    within you?

Is not every continent work'd over and over with sour
    dead?

The earth in the aftermath of the Civil War held the
remains of some eight hundred thousand people killed in
the fighting, and Whitman's voluntary service to wounded
soldiers in the hospitals of the nation's capital had brought
him face to face with the tragic costs of internecine warfare, forcing him to modify his optimistic vision of the
American experiment in liberty. What emerged in his
new poems, in his revisions of "Song of Myself," and in his
prose, particularly *Memoranda During the War*, was the
philosophical grid within which many modern poets operate, including Roethke, A. R. Ammons, Galway Kinnell,
and Mark Strand, all of whom shaped my thinking. On
the mantel of my grandparents' house in Maryland was a
bloodstained bullet chiseled out of a tree on the battlefield
at Gettysburg. I liked to roll it between my fingers as a
child, imagining what it would have been like to fight on
the Union side, little knowing that someday I would find
myself reporting on the wars of succession in the former

Yugoslavia. There I would learn firsthand why people raise arms against their fellow citizens, repudiating what Whitman celebrated in his preface to the first edition of *Leaves of Grass*: "The messages of great poets to each man and woman are, Come to us on equal terms, Only then can you understand us, We are no better than you, What we enclose you enclose, What we enjoy you may enjoy." The bloodshed compelled the first great American poet to revise his ideas about his country's future, demanding more freedom, equality, and fraternity, ever mindful of the consequences of failure. "Where have you disposed of their carcasses?" he asks in "This Compost," knowing that if he were to press his spade into the sod and turn it over he would "expose some of the foul meat."

What I was learning in the nursery, in the life cycles of flowers and trees, in our dependence on sunlight and water, in the beauty of landscape designs that imitate patterns found in nature, is that poetry grows from the soil, like the dogwood tree, my totem. Jerry's malicious gesture was of a piece with what we all do to the earth, generating garbage, polluting the air and water, and burning fossil fuels, which heat the atmosphere, melt icepacks, raise sea levels. The foreman chastised Jerry before we pushed the truck out of the mud, and from the look of contrition on his face I suspected that he would not pull such a stunt again. Individuals and nations have the capacity to self-correct, and as the tires spun I realized that this was the sort of juncture at which one either comes to one's senses or continues down the road to destruction.

It so happened that I was approaching my own turning point, which I should have foreseen. Ordered to eradicate slugs in the nursery, I spent three days mixing batches of a sweet-smelling pesticide to spray under the trees and tables of flowers, along the paths, and around the greenhouse—all without bothering to wear gloves or a mask. The lump I discovered in my neck at Christmas I attributed to my carelessness with the poison, which must have seeped into my body. When I wrote about this in *Things of the Hidden God: Journey to the Holy Mountain*, treating the matter through the lens of a spiritual crisis, I left out a detail about my recovery from surgery to excise the tumor and several swollen lymph nodes—which proved to be benign. Recuperating at a friend's house in Kirkland, my head swathed in bandages like a turban, I set off on foot one sunlit morning for the nursery, a walk of more than a mile, because I wanted to see my friends, to wander among the blooming azaleas and camellias, to smell the fragrance of bark and flowers—to be in a place, that is, devoted to growing things.

I thought: this is my home.

Spike

The master gardener program offered through the agricultural extension service met weekly during my last winter in Salt Lake City. Five years had passed since my surgery, during which I had fallen in love, married, and moved to Utah for a doctoral program in creative writing, and now I was attending lectures on botany, soil science, irrigation, landscape design, and pruning methods. In a green binder were fact sheets on flowers and trees, fruits and vegetables, fertilizers and pesticides, which I studied more intently than the reading list for my comprehensive exams. Among my fellow master gardener students were laborers and contractors who, like me, sought knowledge and marketable skills. For my decision to continue my graduate education, which was putting a strain on my marriage, had turned out to be disastrous.

It was at a Christmas party—on the very night of my discovering the tumor in my neck—that a beautiful violinist came into my life. Lisa was dressed in black, fresh from a performance of Handel's *Messiah*, and I was smitten. Our courtship did not begin, however, until after my surgery. One spring morning I looked out the window and saw her lying upside down on my neighbor's front steps, as if she had slipped and fallen: it was a practical joke played on her friend, who feared she had broken her neck. Lisa's quirky sense of humor charmed me during our whirlwind romance, which took us to Middlebury for the summer and fall, where I coached the B soccer team, then back to Seattle, where we married the following spring. The University of Utah had offered me a fellowship, and though Lisa dreaded the prospect of living in the desert after the lushness of the Northwest, she went along with my decision to accept it; from the day of our arrival in Salt Lake City, when she wept at the sight of the dry brown mountains above the campus, we struggled to regain the lightheartedness that had first brought us together.

My disenchantment with the writing program did not help matters. Workshop rivalries left me reeling, the seminars bored me, and since I refused to curry favor with my professors I grew increasingly isolated. My only consolation was being outdoors—hiking and cross-country skiing in the Wasatch Range, exploring Canyonlands and

Zion, gardening. A doctor from the VA hospital gave me steady landscaping work, and by the time I finished the master gardener program I thought that if all else failed I could make a living working on the land.

Which was what I chose to do when the head of my PhD committee, a celebrated poet with a serious cocaine problem, called me into his office the week after my exams to inform me that in the committee's view I had written at insufficient length and specificity to qualify for the degree. His colleagues, he added, believed that with six months of supervised study I would probably ace the exams on the next try. But I could see no reason to retake them, certain that this black mark on my record would prevent me from ever finding an academic job.

"You had one chance to give me a degree," I said with contempt. "Now I'll find out whether I can become a real writer or not."

Lisa was understandably upset. She had long urged me to abandon my studies. The master's degree in performance she earned from the university was for her a holding action—and a source of constant irritation between us. Now this.

"What are we going to do?" she asked.

In the morning I got up to write—I did not know what

else to do—and when I had finished a page of a short story I headed for the doctor's house, in the foothills above the city, to work in the garden, a routine I followed for several weeks. With few exceptions, my classmates from the writing program kept their distance, not knowing, perhaps, what to say. Lisa and I spent our nights debating what to do and where to go. It was a lonely time.

In May, with the doctor's blessing, I began to clear a grove of scrub oaks above the rock wall at the edge of her backyard, intending to plant fruit and ornamental trees, including flowering dogwoods. Scrub oaks (*Quercus gambelii*) have dense, gnarly wood, and the work was slow going, requiring frequent stops to oil and sharpen the chainsaw. One classmate, a poet from Georgia, had reached out to me in friendship, so I hired him to help. We found a good rhythm, with him pushing or pulling on the trees to give me a better angle for cutting, and when we took a break I was surprised to see how much space had opened up. The sky was clear, and the sunlight filtering through the leaves made a play of shadows on the ground, which pleased me as I tightened the chain. My friend asked what my plans were for the future.

I shrugged. "This, I guess."

It took us a while to get going again, and for some

reason the next tree I selected was particularly hard to fell. My friend was reaching for another branch when the chainsaw struck a rusted spike embedded in its trunk and bucked in my hands, slashing his thigh. He did not flinch or speak, and it was not until he peeled back the flap of his torn jeans to reveal blood spurting from a wound, which would require several stiches, that I saw how close I had come to maiming him. He was remarkably calm, despite what must have been great pain, and he did not seem to blame me for my carelessness. Indeed his stoicism is what I remember most vividly about those anxious weeks when Lisa and I were trying to figure out our lives. In a level voice he said, "We need to get to the hospital." After that day I left the rest of the trees standing.

Calendaring

A fourteen-volume edition of Henry David Thoreau's *Journal* came into my possession as partial payment for a freelance editing job, around the time that Lisa and I moved to New Mexico to work as caretakers of an estate on the edge of the Santa Fe National Forest. It was my custom in the morning to read a page or two of Thoreau's entries before I started writing, which not only eased my way into the work at hand but also trained my eye to notice the flora and fauna of my new surroundings in the high desert—piñon pines and cottonwoods, rabbitbrush and sage, coyotes and black bears, dippers and towhees and magpies. Thoreau's achievement in *Walden* and other works is rooted in his powers of observation, which developed to such an extent that the practice of attention became his principal literary mode. Of his home ground in Massachusetts he wrote, "I think I could write a poem to be called Concord," which would include the river and ponds, woods and hills, fields and swamps and meadows, as well as the streets and buildings and villagers. This is precisely what he created in his *Journal*, which filled forty-seven manuscript volumes: a meticulous record of his excursions near and far. "I have traveled much in Concord," he wrote, gathering material for his lectures, essays, and books. Working as a land surveyor, a vocation that allowed him to indulge his passion for botanizing, Thoreau made field notes on his morning rambles, learning the textures of his chosen place so well that if he had fallen into a slumber lasting for years, upon awakening, he believed, he would be able to determine the date within a day or two based on which plants were flowering. How to gain such knowledge, such wisdom, except by paying attention?

References to dogwoods—flowering, grey, red osier, silky, alternate- and round-leaved, bunchberry, dwarf— take up more than a page of the botanical index to the *Journal*. Thoreau's method is on display in the following pair of entries, which, in addition to documenting the progress of the season and speculating about the ways of nature, highlight the fact that dogwoods, like every element of every ecosystem, do not exist in a vacuum:

5 A.M. - To Island by boat.

Everything has sensibly advanced during the warm and
moist night. Some trees, as the small maples in the street,
already look verdurous. The air has not sensibly cooled
much. The chimney swallows are busily skimming low
over the river and just touching the water without regard
to me, as a week ago they did, and as they circle back
overhead to repeat the experiment, I hear a sharp snap
or short rustling of their wings. The button-bush now
shows the first signs of life, on a close inspection, in its
small round, smooth, greenish buds. The polygonums and
pontederias are getting above water, the latter like spoons
on long handles. The *Cornus florida* is blossoming; will be
fairly out to-day. The *Polygonatum pubescens*; one on the
Island has just opened. This is the smaller Solomon's-seal.
A thorn there will blossom to-day. The *Viola palmata* is
out there, in the meadow. Everywhere the huckleberry's
sticky leaves are seen expanding, and the *high blueberry*
is in blossom. Now is the time to admire the very young
and tender leaves. The blossoms of the red oak hang down
under its young leaves as under a canopy. The petals have
already fallen from the *Amelanchier Botryapium*, and
young berries are plainly forming. I hear the wood pewee,

— *pe-a-wai*. The heat of yesterday has brought him on. [May 17, 1853]

Cornus Canadensis blooms apparently with *C. florida*; not *quite* yet. I mistook dense groves of little barberries in the droppings of cows in the Boulder Field for apple trees at first. So the cows eat barberries, and help disperse or disseminate them exactly as they do the apple! That helps account for the spread of the barberry, then. See the genista, winter-killed at top, some seven or eight rods north of the southernmost large boulder in the Boulder Field. Cannot find any large corydalis plants where it has been very plenty. A few of the *Cornus florida* buds by the pond have escaped after all. [May 29, 1858]

In another entry, May 22, 1856, Thoreau notes, "The *Cornus florida* does not bloom this year." Indeed the eighth volume of his *Journal* contains almost no references to dogwoods—a sign of things to come. For Harvard University researchers studying his inventory of plants near Walden Pond concluded, in 2008, that climate change has drastically altered his beloved landscape. *Science Daily* reports that plants flower on average one week earlier than in Thoreau's time, and while some nonnative plants thrive in the warmer weather, the majority have not adapted to the 2.3° Celsius (4.3° Fahrenheit) rise in average annual temperature since 1854, when *Walden* was published; more than a quarter of the species listed in his works have vanished from the area, and another third are on the verge of local extinction, including lilies, orchids, buttercups, roses, violets, mints, and dogwoods. If by some miracle Thoreau were reincarnated in Concord he would not be able to guess the date. And he would be appalled by the number of pages missing from the Book of Nature, which he read and interpreted so well that generations of writers, artists, and naturalists have learned from him how to vividly describe landscapes; discern patterns in the natural world—of flowering and fruiting and migration; appreciate the beauty of what the Roman philosopher Pliny the Elder called "the least things of nature." But Concord's native plant list has been so depleted by warming temperatures that it is as if a great fire swept through the area, destroying the natural diversity that captivated Thoreau. Some visitors to Walden Pond are disappointed by its meager aspect—which cannot be blamed entirely on the discrepancy between reality and the vision of the place built up in the imagination of *Walden*'s readers. The entries in his *Journal* are thus elegiac, poignant reminders of what was once a thriving ecosystem, like artifacts unearthed from the volcanic ash that buried Pompeii. We have squandered our natural inheritance.

"The species harmed by climate change are among the most charismatic found in the New England landscape," said Charles C. Davis, an evolutionary biology professor and lead author of the Harvard study. In a separate study published in 2010 he observed that "groups of related species are being selectively trimmed from the Tree of Life, rather than individual species being randomly pruned from its tips." His results indicate that the local extinction in Concord, which may underlie global extinction, is commensurate with the fossil record of the previous five mass extinctions. Invasive species may benefit most from the climate change central to the sixth mass extinction: as the planet warms, and dogwoods give way to desert, monotony will reign.

In New Mexico I found nothing monotonous about my work as a caretaker—gardening in the beds of roses, wildflowers, vegetables, and perennials; planting bulbs and raking leaves in the fall; splitting wood for the winter and repairing tools; pruning trees in spring. These tasks formed a vital counterpoint to my literary activities, my inner life, what the poet William Matthews called "this quarantine, / reading and pacing and feeding the fireplace." Stoking the woodstove on a cold October morning, I heard a red-shafted flicker drumming on the wooden beam, the viga, above the door of our adobe cottage, which had once served as a chicken coop. A magpie glided through the apple orchard. The golden leaves of the quaking aspens shone on the hillside across the canyon. I opened Thoreau's *Journal* to the day's date in 1860 and read, "I see not one hemlock cone of this year at the Hemlocks, but very many of last year holding on. Apparently they bore so abundantly last year that they do not bear at all this year." But now comes word from scientists at the University of Massachusetts that the eastern hemlock, the so-called redwood of the East, a majestic conifer that can live eight hundred years or more, may vanish from New England forests by the end of the century, because of climate change and the ravages of a sap-sucking insect accidently introduced decades ago from Japan, the hemlock wooly adelgid, which has laid waste to hemlock groves from the southern Appalachians to Connecticut. Only frigid weather seems to slow its rate of destruction, and the milder winters are expanding its range northward. What would Thoreau say?

The Forgotten Language

Walking the acequia was my favorite springtime ritual. This community-based irrigation system, dating back to the Moorish conquest of Spain, was brought to the Southwest by Spanish settlers in the sixteenth century, and the watercourse running through Little Tesuque Canyon is maintained according to the old ways. My neighbors, their hired help, and I would gather at the *toma*, the point of diversion from Little Tesuque Creek at the edge of the Santa Fe National Forest, and then head downstream, removing leaves and branches and brush from the channel so that the apple orchards could be irrigated without interruption. During the growing season, each landowner was allotted a set number of minutes of water per week, which pooled around the trees, where at dawn or dusk you might see coyotes or brown bears. Red osier dogwoods, also known as creek dogwoods, had been planted among the cottonwoods along portions of the acequia to stem erosion, and I relished their thickets of bright red stems, which provide cover for birds, food for deer and smaller mammals, and ingredients for basket weaving and dyes used by Native Americans, who make tinctures and poultices from the bark to treat a variety of ailments—hemorrhages, headaches, sore eyes, afterbirth complications, rashes, diarrhea, fevers and pains, fear and paranoia.

A neighbor joked that we had the best-managed acequia in northern New Mexico, because our majordomo, Percival King, had worked on the Manhattan Project. Since his retirement from Los Alamos National Laboratory (his inventions included the catalytic recombiner for a nuclear reactor, which mixes radiological gases and also serves as a safety valve), he had tended his orchard, monitored the acequia, caught raccoons in a Havahart trap. One year he trapped the same raccoon over and over, each time loading it into his car and then driving up into the Sangre de Cristo Mountains to release it; the joke my neighbors told was that some days the raccoon made it back to his house before he did. It was strange to think of an atomic bomb–maker taking pity on a varmint.

The threat of nuclear holocaust seemed acute in those days, with the Soviet army mired in Afghanistan and the Reagan administration building up armed forces, deploying MX and Pershing missiles, and launching the Strategic Defense Initiative, also known as Star Wars. The Cold War was heating up; the fear was general that a misstep could bring the superpowers into direct conflict; and in his book *The Fate of the Earth* (1982), Jonathan Schell articulated the dread I sometimes felt at dusk, gazing westward from the mesa behind our house at the lights of Los Alamos. The absurdity of the military doctrine of Mutually Assured Destruction (MAD), which proposed that the prospect of mutual annihilation would dissuade adversaries from using nuclear weapons, became tangible for me in Schell's description of an irradiated planet after nuclear war, in a chapter titled "The Republic of Insects and Grass": millions upon millions of casualties, contaminated food and water supplies, clouds of dust circling the globe for months, withering vegetation, the depletion of the ozone layer. "The machinery of destruction is complete," he wrote, "poised on a hair trigger, waiting for the 'button' to be 'pushed' by some misguided or deranged human being or for some faulty computer chip to send out the instruction to fire. That so much should be balanced on so fine a point—that the fruit of four and a half billion years can be undone in a careless moment—is a fact against which belief rebels." Wading in the cool water of the acequia on an April morning, I was struck by the fragility of everything I held dear: how easily the invention of the old man forking wet leaves out of the acequia could spell the end of life as we know it.

This was why I founded the Taos Conference on Writing and the Natural World, which ran for three years, bringing together writers and naturalists to explore different ways of addressing our relationship to the environment. The conference took place at Fort Burgwin, a research center belonging to Southern Methodist University; the irony of meeting in a restored cantonment, built in 1852 to fend off Utes and Jicarilla Apaches and named after an officer killed in the Mexican-American War, was lost on no one. W. S. Merwin, the featured poet at the last conference, in the fall of 1991, reminded participants that Thoreau's essay "On Civil Disobedience" stemmed from his opposition to slavery and the Mexican-American War. After his arrest and jailing for refusing to pay his poll taxes, Thoreau laid out a philosophical argument for withdrawing support from an unjust government—which inspired Mahatma Gandhi and Martin Luther King Jr. to create the passive resistance movements critical to, respectively, India securing its independence from the British Empire and the American battle for civil rights. The looming environmental catastrophe demanded nothing less from us, Merwin declared. We were sitting in a circle at the edge of a meadow where Indian paintbrush and scarlet trumpet bloomed; under the golden spell of aspens Merwin's poem "Second Witness" guided our discussions about the writer's role in this crisis:

> I want to tell what the forests
> were like
>
> I will have to speak
> in a forgotten language

Learning to speak that language, he suggested, on the page and by example, was our most urgent task. The destruction of the natural order represented for him a new form of the final solution, the Nazi program to exterminate Jews in Europe. Our forebears' failure to save the Jews in World War II must not be repeated in the war on the environment, or all would be lost.

After the conference, William and his wife, Paula, stayed in our guesthouse for a night before flying home. The gardens in my care prompted his invitation to housesit for them during his next reading tour: he needed someone to tend to his botanical preserve in Maui—nineteen acres

of a former pineapple plantation, on which he was growing more than seven hundred species of palm trees, many
of them endangered or extinct in the wild—and so each
spring for the next several years I spent a month or more
in the solar-powered house he had designed himself and
helped to build. There I harvested strawberry bananas
from the grove by the nursery in which palm seedlings
grew, cared for a quartet of temperamental chow chows,
read his work and that of other writers who had influenced
him. His advice to me in Santa Fe—"Try to maintain your
independence for as long as you can"—acquired a tangible
form in his library and garden. He had chosen to live de-
liberately, in the kind of solitude that Thoreau would have
appreciated. In Maui I tried to follow his example.

"What more can you do?" he asks in the last lines
of "Unchopping a Tree," a prose parable collected in *The
Miner's Pale Children* (1970). Composed in the form of a
set of instructions for raising a felled tree, it records the
steps of a hopelessly heartbreaking operation: the leaves,
twigs, nests, and spiders' webs that must be gathered up,
to say nothing of the branches, splintered trunk, and bark;
the care that must be exercised in raising the tackle or
scaffolding; the adhesives applied, which hold together
ships and sawdust; and then the moment when "the last

sustaining piece is removed and the tree stands again on its own. It is as though its weight for a moment stood on your heart." The narrator wonders how long it will stand—and if he has forgotten anything.

"But there is nothing more for you to do," he realizes in the end. "Others are waiting. Everything is going to have to be put back."

Merwin's project, through scores of books of poetry, prose, and translations, has been to try to put everything back. His is a lifelong essay in restoration—of personal and poetic freedom, of ways of seeing and hearing, of a ruined house in France and a pineapple field in Maui. Born in 1927 in New York City, the son of a Presbyterian minister for whom he wrote hymns as a boy, he was raised in Union City, New Jersey, and Scranton, Pennsylvania, and from an early age he seemed always to have been aware of the encroachments of industrial society. One of his first memories, in fact, was of running into his backyard to scream at the telephone repairmen who were chopping limbs off a favorite poplar tree. That cry he transformed into literary work.

As a student at Princeton Merwin visited Ezra Pound at St. Elizabeth's Hospital in Washington, D.C., and took the elder poet's advice to write seventy-five lines a day, to

"read seeds, not twigs," to use his gift for learning languages to translate. After graduation and a stint on Ma-
jorca as the tutor to Robert Graves's children, he turned to
translation to support himself, choosing a different path
from his contemporaries, living frugally in New York and
London, in France and Mexico, and finally in Maui. "It
seems to me," he told an interviewer, "that in so far as a
man prizes some spring of independence—independence
from the cant of economics and the tyranny of history—in
himself, the hope of being fully human, which is integral
to all poetry, remains alive." Translating freed him from
the shackles of academic life; the works he brought into
English—which included French and Spanish poetry and
prose, Asian proverbs, aboriginal chants, Dante's *Purga-
torio*, *Sir Gawain and the Green Knight*, and the doomed
Russian poet Osip Mandelstam's curse against Stalin ("He
rolls the executions on his tongue like berries")—opened
new ways for him to hear his own language.

Which opened my ears, too. I followed his example
as a translator, beginning with André Breton's last original book, *Constellations* (1959)—twenty-two prose poems
based on Joan Miró's series of gouaches completed in
1941. A French scholar, Jeanie Puleston Fleming, agreed
to help me in the pleasurable task of Englishing poems

with titles like "Beautiful Bird Deciphering the Unknown for Two Lovers" and "On the 13th the Ladder Grazed the Heavens." Breton was impelled to write about the gouaches, according to the Mexican poet Octavio Paz, for both aesthetic and ethical reasons—aesthetic because the unity and energy of the series "struck him as one of the *happiest* moments of Miró's life work," and ethical because it "literally *illuminated* the obscure relationships between history and artistic creation." He continued,

> Miró had painted these rather small-sized gouaches at a terrible moment in his life and modern history: Spain under Franco's dictatorship, Europe occupied by the Nazis, his poet and painter friends persecuted in France or in exile in America. The appearance in those dark, gloomy days of a work that is a fountain of colors and living forms was an answer to the pressure of history.

Miró's exuberant response to the enveloping darkness reminded Paz that "the earth always answers humanity's insults with spring greetings. Perhaps art is only the expression of the tragic joy of existence." The same held for Merwin's work. The marriage of aesthetics and ethics was what gave it such force—and what I hoped to achieve in my own writing. A line from *Constellations* would run through my mind when I walked in his garden: "The mountain ash enters the lyre, or else the lyre enters the ash." The inextricable link in my imagination between nature and poetry grew stronger with each day that I spent at Merwin's house.

"What you remember saves you," he proclaims in "Learning a Dead Language." What he remembered at every turn was humankind's despoiling of the world. His environmental writings went hand in hand with his support for the nuclear disarmament movement and his outrage at the war in Indochina. In his 1967 collection of poems *The Lice*, a complex dirge for the whole of life, he gave voice to the voiceless, the nonhuman world that surrounds and sustains us. "Among my peculiar failings," he once said,

> is an inability to believe that the experience of being human, that gave rise to the arts in the first place, can continue to be nourished in a world contrived and populated by nothing but humans. No doubt such a situation is biologically impossible, but it is economically desirable, and we exist in an era dedicated to the myth that the biology of the planet, as well as anything else that may be, can be forced to adapt infinitely to the appetites of our species, organized and deified under the name of economics.

This "peculiar failing" led him to restore a patch of land above a sea cliff on the eastern, or windward, coast of Maui. The original forest of Hawaiian koas, 'ōhi'a lehuas, and other native species had been reduced since the 1840s to what the state agricultural agency pronounced a wasteland. First the trees were cut down to provide firewood for whaling ships and American and European settlers, creating pasture for cattle to graze on the wild grasses; then sugarcane farmers diverted water from the stream running through the valley; and then pineapple growers, plowing the slopes vertically instead of horizontally, completed the destruction, as winter rains carried the last of the topsoil away. The fields were abandoned, and by the time Merwin walked over the dry grass all that remained were some scraggly guavas and Christmas berries, an imported weed tree. "The wind blowing across the ridge behind me framed the silence," he recalled in a summary written for the Nature Conservancy, "The House and Garden: The Emergence of a Dream." And when he heard plovers sailing overhead in pairs, "the same clear, rising notes that they called to each other on their long migration flights at night over the sea," the place captured his imagination. He likened the sound to the tolling of a bell, which summoned him to attend.

On the day he signed his papers for the property, in 1977, and nearly every day thereafter he planted a tree, determined to restore some portion of pure Hawaiian rainforest. But as no native trees would grow in such parched conditions, in leached-out soil, he planted casuarinas, a nonnative species known locally as ironwoods, which grew quickly, provided shade, added humus to the soil, and served as a nitrogen fixative. This created a microclimate along the ridge, which in time made it possible for him to plant native species, beginning with Hawaiian palms. But he did not realize that termites had evolved to attack ironwoods when they reach a certain height; pieces of wood, thick with termites, had lately started falling out of the trees. The palms he was planting to replace them were but a foot tall. Then again the ironwoods shading the road had been no taller when he planted them long ago. Restoration demands patience.

"I learned how many native Hawaiian things you could not put back on the place where they originally grew, because the disturbance was so great," he told me. "This idea that you can reforest is nonsense. You can't reforest. It's like saying you're going to replant medieval society somewhere in Canada just by putting in a few cathedrals and a few odds and ends. The whole symbiotic connection is of an infinite complexity we don't begin to understand. We don't know. The forest is hundreds of species and things, all related to each other. It's a highly intricate society. The forest knows how to do it. We know how to plant trees and hope that it establishes a relationship—if we plant the right trees in the right places."

A place apart—this was what he wanted to create in Maui. And this was what I felt there. The ancient link between poetry and nature was manifested both in the garden—where seedlings from around the world grew into tall palm trees that hid the sea from view—and in my conversations with Merwin, who insisted on the sacredness of our vocation. "The poet's role," he explained one afternoon, "is always the same, which is to talk about seeing life whole—trying to see it whole, to hear it whole, trying to hear what makes it complete, what makes a painting of three persimmons represent the entire world, because every work of art says, This is complete. If you can really look at this, if you can really hear this, you'll hear everything."

Sometimes at dinner, after a glass or two of wine, he would recite passages from *In Parenthesis*, David Jones's epic poem about his service as an infantryman with the Royal Welsh Fusiliers in World War I, in the trenches in

France and then at the Battle of the Somme, where more than a million men were killed or wounded, including Jones himself. His exploration of British and Welsh mythology fascinated Merwin, who had reason to believe he was himself a descendant of Merlin, the wizard of Arthurian legend, and he loved the language of the poem, which seemed to him to rise from some deep well of the race, a mixture of verse and prose thick with echoes of Shakespeare, Malory, ancient prayers and battle cries, laws and codes of conduct dating to the Roman occupation of Britain.

What fired my imagination was Jones's pledge "to make a shape in words, using as data the complex sights, sounds, fears, hopes, apprehensions, smells, things exterior and interior, the landscape and paraphernalia of that singular time and of those particular men." Unclassifiable, this shape, comprising different registers of diction ranging from high to low, often within the same paragraph, captured "the sudden violences and the long stillnesses" of the battlefield, which was for him "a place of enchantment." Jones trained my ear to another music, and his description of shellfire—"As though the Behemoth stirred from the moist places, tensored his brass sinews suddenly, shattered with deep-bellied trumpetings the long quietude; awaking stench and earthquake in his burrowing-up"—prepared me for what I would experience in the coming years in Bosnia. The war zone and Merwin's garden tutored me in different ways. When I went to bed in Maui, my sleep was marked by the sound of palm fronds crashing to the ground, which bore a resemblance to the artillery rounds that would regularly awaken me during the siege of Sarajevo.

Besieged

Like Thoreau, I tried to "live at home like a traveler," little knowing that I was about to embark on a series of journeys to the far corners of the world, which would complicate my idea of home. My wife wanted to return to the Northwest, where she could find more work as a musician than in New Mexico, and so we gave notice to the owners of the estate, packed up our things, and moved to Portland. In our first year there I wrote a book about World Cup soccer in Italy, then set off to cover the wars of succession in the former Yugoslavia. Our Portland flat was close to Washington Park, and when I had finished writing for the day I would go for a run along its wooded trails, stopping to rest by either the Japanese stone-and-sand garden or the memorial to Vietnam War veterans, the Garden of Solace, where kousa dogwoods bloomed in spring and the scarlet bark of Siberian dogwoods (*Cornus alba*) mesmerized in winter. Freed from my desk, I breathed the fresh air, in rain and sunshine, letting my mind wander over what I had witnessed abroad and unearthed in research, seeking connections between one thing and another.

This ritual I maintained when we moved into a bungalow at the edge of Mount Tabor Park, an extinct volcanic cinder cone surrounded by nearly two hundred acres of forests and reservoirs. I would run past redwoods and cedars, pines and spruces, magnolias and dogwoods (*Cornus nuttallii* and *Cornus mas*—the European cornel, last glimpsed on a hike in Slovenia, not far from a mountain hut crowded with refugees from Bosnia), puzzling out the structure of a book about the war, which would claim 150,000 lives and send millions more into exile.

In the spring of 1993, after traveling in the Balkans for the better part of a year, I boarded a military transport plane in Split, Croatia, a humanitarian flight bound for the besieged city of Sarajevo. I had hundreds of pages of notes—and no idea how to write a book, the advance for which I was rapidly spending. "Maybe Airlines" was what UN peacekeepers called the airlift destined to eclipse the Berlin airlift in length and scope, and on this C-130 peacekeepers, humanitarians, and journalists were crammed against crates of food and medicine. The plane made an assault landing at Butmir Airport, the front line between government and Serbian forces, then taxied quickly past the wreckage of another military transport plane to the terminal, which was surrounded by sandbags and barbed wire. There I climbed into an armored personnel carrier (APC) for the drive into the capital of Bosnia-Herzegovina, which had no natural gas, water, or electricity. It was stifling in the crowded APC; the soldiers at each checkpoint took their time going through our papers. Twisted shells of buildings rose above the Miljacka River flowing through the center of town. Cars sped along Sniper Alley, where all manner of shields had been raised—dumpsters, slabs of concrete, sheets of rusted iron—to offer some protection to pedestrians, who ran or walked swiftly across open intersections with their heads down.

A year into the longest siege in modern history, Sarajevo was a shattered place. Serbian gunners in the surrounding hills rained down a thousand shells a day into the city, damaging or destroying nearly every building; snipers shot civilians, including women and children, with astonishing regularity. For food, Sarajevans relied on the airlift and the black market. It was a desperate situation, not least because the arms embargo that the international community had imposed on Yugoslavia all but prevented the ragtag Bosnian forces from defending the city. Thus gallows humor reigned. One joke making the rounds was particularly dark: What is the difference between Auschwitz and Sarajevo? At least in Auschwitz they had gas.

It was an open secret that the Bosnians would soon try to break the siege, and when the uneasy calm that reigned during my first days in the city ended early one Saturday morning in a hail of shellfire, I followed several humanitarians into the basement of their rented house: a familiar refuge for Sarajevans in those days. No telling how long we might have to stay there. Terrified, I took notes, not because I expected to turn them into a piece of writing but because the act of documenting the event calmed me. I recorded almost every conversation, story, and joke; described my surroundings in minute detail; timed the interval between the rare outgoing *pop* of a Bosnian grenade and the ensuing blizzard of Serbian shells. When I went to sleep that night, in makeshift conditions, I had a fairly complete set of notes from one day of life in a basement under fire.

I also had severe spasms in my back, having wrenched it during a lull in the bombardment. I had gone upstairs to get some air, and when I stepped out onto the balcony to survey the damage a sniper shot at me, the bullet lodging in the lintel above the door. I dove back inside, awkwardly twisting in my Kevlar vest, the heavy weight of which tore a band of muscles in my lower back—an injury that turned out to be a blessing in disguise. In the morning, barely able to walk, I caught a humanitarian flight to Split, on the Adriatic Sea, intending to return to Sarajevo after I had recuperated. No sooner did I reach my hotel, though, than I began to shake uncontrollably. Nerves, I thought, climbing into bed, where I fell asleep, chilled to the bone, only to wake some hours later drenched in sweat.

"Typhus," said the doctor who took my temperature in the morning—106°. "Maybe war dysentery. I don't think you'll die," she added. "Then again you might not want to believe me."

Hours passed before I was admitted to a military hospital, by which time I was delirious. What I remember of the next several days is the pleasure the nurses seemed to take in letting my intravenous bottles run dry. I was sharing a room with two convalescing Croatian soldiers, who liked to watch my arm swell—or so I imagined, since only they could convince the nurses to bring me a new bottle, and they sometimes waited an hour or more to call for help.

This went on for three days before my fever broke. It was in the wee hours of the morning that music from a radio in another room awoke me, the title track of Dire

Straits' *Brother in Arms*: "Every man has to die," Mark Knopfler sang, and when he launched into a haunting guitar solo a wave of relief washed over me. I had heard the song only once before, six months earlier, on a crackly sound system in the darkening corridor of a hotel in Dubrovnik, after spending a day in a village razed by paramilitaries, and now, in a hospital farther up the coast, the music struck me with particular force. I had a vision—there is no other word for it—of how to organize my as-yet unwritten book. My pain dissolved as I lay in the dark, buoyantly plotting out a triptych of the Balkan wars: the opening section would be set in Slovenia, the first Yugoslav republic to win independence; the second would recount my journey through Croatia, Serbia, Montenegro, Kosovo, Macedonia, and the surrounding countries of Austria, Bulgaria, Greece, and Turkey; the third would tell the story of the war in Bosnia, beginning in the basement, where Sarajevans had spent so many days and nights.

To give readers a sense of daily life under siege, I would devote a chapter to the events and conversations I had chronicled in the basement: the thud of artillery and the fragrance of flowers in a vase; stories of atrocities committed by Serbian troops, of an adventure at the front, of heroism; debates about war crimes, military strategy, humanitarian principles, the international community's failure to end the bloodshed, what to read during a bombardment; memories of food, wine, music; a guard's confession that he tape-recorded the moans of his lovers. This was a war waged largely against civilians—the joke in Sarajevo was that if you were in the army you had a better chance of surviving than noncombatants—and I intended to give voice to some of the victims. Their testimony would be the compass for a travelogue through a modern hell, the contours of which might become clear in the course of writing.

My euphoria had worn off by daybreak, and months would pass before I was well enough to return to Sarajevo. My travels in the war zones of Bosnia and Herzegovina were just beginning, and I knew that my interviews on all sides of the conflict would leave me feeling lost if I did not learn to hold in mind competing narratives. To gain insight into this troubled part of the world, I would read widely in history and literature, political theory and theology; consult humanitarians, civil-society experts, military monitors; test ideas in public forums. More danger, bewilderment, and sorrow lay ahead of me. But I had glimpsed the outlines of a book. Page by page, at my desk and in the woods around the volcano, I would try to heal myself.

A Route of Evanescence

On the Double Ninth Festival, a Chinese holiday observed on the ninth day of the ninth month on the lunar calendar, families wearing sashes of dogwood leaves and berries climb mountains and then drink chrysanthemum wine— a ritual to ward off misfortune. Chongyang (Double Nine) is based on the philosophical theory of yin and yang, yin being the feminine or negative principle of the universe, yang the male or positive principle—the duality (light and dark, fire and water) that lies at the heart of existence. Nine is a yang number, and in this system of complementary forces, where everything possesses yin and yang elements, the conjunction of two yang numbers carries the risk of danger, which may be mitigated by ritual, as well as the promise of longevity, if danger can be avoided. Chongyang is thus a warning to remain vigilant and a symbol of both possibility and completeness, the perfect life being "a little less than enough," according to Taoist thinkers. Hence the number nine, not ten, is cause for celebration.

There are two versions of the legend explaining the birth of the rituals observed on Chongyang, both involving a man named Huan Jing. During the Eastern Han dynasty (AD 25–220), he studied the art of magic with a Taoist said to be immortal, Fei Changfang, whom Huan believed might teach him how to slay the river monster that brought pestilence to his village every fall. They were climbing a mountain on the eighth day of the ninth lunar month, when Fei stopped in his tracks to warn Huan that disaster was imminent. In one telling of the story, Fei urged Huan to hurry home, make a red bag adorned with a spray of dogwood leaves for each villager, and lead them up the mountain as they held cups of chrysanthemum wine. When the monster appeared at noon, the fragrance of dogwood and chrysanthemum (used in Chinese medicine to drive away evil spirits and cure the sick) distracted it long enough for Huan to cut it down with a sword Fei had given him. In another telling, Huan heeded his master's instructions to take his family up the mountain; upon his return that evening, he found his chickens, sheep, dogs, and oxen dead of pestilence—sacrificed, so it seemed, in order to save him and his family. (No other villagers survived.) The custom of climbing a mountain on Chong-yang became an official festival during the Tang dynasty (618–690, 705–907), giving rise to a tradition of Double Nine poems, the most famous of which was composed by Wang Wei (701–761) on the theme of exile, translated here by David Hinton:

9/9, THINKING OF MY BROTHERS EAST OF THE MOUNTAINS

Each year on this auspicious day, alone and foreign
here in a foreign place, my thoughts of you sharpen:

far away, I can almost see you reaching the summit,
dogwood berries woven into sashes, short one person.

In the fall of 2001, my best friend, the poet Agha Shahid Ali, was dying of brain cancer. His vision was skewed, his memory dissolving (the events of 9/11 he referred to as "that thing that happened in New York"), and yet until his final days he could recite reams of poetry, including the whole of Milton's "Lycidas," an elegy of nearly two hundred lines for a drowned Cambridge classmate. This caught the attention of the neurologist Oliver Sacks, author of *Awakenings* and other best-selling books on the workings of the mind, who examined him to better understand the poetic imagination. I read Sacks's notes on the case within days of Shahid's oncologist determining that nothing more could be done for him, and in the midst of my grief I marveled at the endurance, and vitality, of the connections my friend had forged in poetry.

Shahid defined himself as a triple exile—from his native Kashmir; from India proper; from Urdu, the language of his childhood—and exile was the theme, secret or overt, of his poems, drafts of which he would read to me over the phone. We called each other almost daily for close to twenty years, sometimes talking for hours—telling jokes, trading stories, commiserating about love and politics, comparing notes on what we were reading or writing. I came to recognize in him a certain restlessness that signaled the imminent arrival of a poem, which he would describe before writing a word, explaining its source—in a dream, an image, a formal imperative—and how it might develop. Then he would read me successive drafts, demanding an authentic response.

"Be honest," he insisted, expecting me not only to identify problems but to offer solutions. And if I pointed out an awkward phrase or an image that was vague he would say, "Oh, darling, I know it doesn't work. Give me another line. Please."

He readily incorporated my suggestions, amending them as needed to suit his ear, which was alert to livelier tones than mine. When I noted that as much as a third of one of his books could be attributed to me, he laughed. "It's all poetry," he said. His was a Platonic ideal of writing: it did not matter how a poem came into being, only that it found its way onto the page.

While I was covering the Balkan wars, he urged me, repeatedly, to turn my attention next to Kashmir, over which India and Pakistan had waged three wars since the end of the British Indian Empire in 1947. He planned to write a novel about a man born at the exact moment of Partition, which had plunged Kashmir into the geopolitical netherworld from which it has yet to emerge; the imagined events in the life of his protagonist, who bore a strong resemblance to him, would intersect at decisive moments with the history of his homeland. Shahid rewrote the opening paragraph many times, and in our last days together, at his brother's house in Amherst, Massachusetts, it occurred to me that his life itself was a novel rich with incident, joy, and grief.

Like anyone, he fictionalized parts of it. He hid his homosexuality from his parents, with whom he was very close, until he was in his thirties; dyed his hair jet black at the first sign of grey; whited out his birth year—1949—on the copyright pages of the books he lavishly inscribed to me. It is a fact, though, that he died on the anniversary of his late mother's first seizure from the same form of cancer that afflicted him, December 8, 2001. State law prevented his family from following the Muslim custom of burying him within twenty-four hours, on a Sunday, so he was interred on Emily Dickinson's birthday, in a cemetery down the road from the house in which she wrote, "If I could bribe them by a Rose / I'd bring them every flower that grows / From Amherst to Cashmere!" These lines furnished the epigraph to his prose poem "'Some Vision of the World Cashmere'"; from her metaphors he learned to map a land of "doomed addresses," articulating a vision of the world that won him a place in American poetry. Another Dickinson line, "A route of Evanescence," inspired the most interesting pages in his book *A Nostalgist's Map of America*. It also describes the arc of our friendship, which from the beginning was shaped by his wit, playfulness, and generosity. Thus at his invitation I celebrated my fortieth birthday in Amherst, the town where I was born, by giving a poetry reading for the creative writing program at the University of Massachusetts, at the conclusion of which his students presented me with a cake.

I am drawn to extravagance, perhaps because I am reticent by nature, and no one in my life was more extravagant than Shahid. He was fond of quoting Oscar Wilde's remark to a customs official that he had nothing to declare but his genius; he knew by heart all of Faye Dunaway's lines in *Mommie Dearest*; his deadpan impersonations of TV commercials—"Fill it to the rim, with Brim," he would say—delighted everyone. When at a dinner party a woman asked if she could lean on his shoulder to speak to a friend seated on the other side of him, he replied, "As so many others have." And when his first visit to us in Santa Fe was delayed by a near disaster, his plane making a crash landing just after takeoff, he said his last thought before impact was that we would not have a drink together that night. He arrived the next day just before I left to teach a workshop at a community college, and Lisa was anxious about entertaining him alone: their initial encounter, at the Bread Loaf Writers' Conference, had not gone well, because he had designs on me. (He had remarkable success in seducing heterosexual men.) He was asleep when I returned, and Lisa was thoroughly charmed, Shahid having explained in considerable detail the complications of sleeping with a well-endowed man. She felt as if she had a new sister. Later he told her his secret regimen for keeping his skin smooth: just before the end of a shower, he would smear baby oil over his entire body and stand there in the steam. When Lisa tried it, she broke out in hives.

"Because you are a white woman," he laughed.

There was a bit of the magpie in him, alert to anything that might be turned into poetry—a casual remark, a joke, a word. For example, this sentence from Thomas De Quincey's *Confessions of an English Opium-Eater*: "It was a year of brilliant water." Not long after telling Shahid that I would use it as the epigraph to a book titled *Brilliant Water*, he made it the epigraph to his poem "In Search of Evanescence," which in addition to lines from Dickinson included titles of paintings and excerpts from the letters of Georgia O'Keeffe. Weaving different voices through his poems, in the manner of one jazz musician quoting another, Shahid created his own form of *brilliant water*, a phrase that became our favorite trope. He mined the writings of others to trigger his imagination (we planned to write a book together titled *The Blond Assassins*, a Dickinson phrase that eventually showed up in his *ghazal* "Forever"), and a partial list of writers appearing in his late poems reveals the breadth of his literary tastes: Mandelstam, Yeats, Gibbon, Hopkins, Shakespeare, Apollinaire, Hafiz, Trakl, Auden, Faiz, Ghalib, Darwish. Quotations provided the scaffolding for his final book, *Call Me Ishmael Tonight*, a collection of ghazals in which he paid homage to American poetry by braiding lines from other poets into his own work. This was Shahid's gift to his adopted homeland: to use the language so well that it acquired a new light, accent, and sense of possibility.

At the age of twelve he moved with his family to Muncie, Indiana (his father earned his doctorate at Ball State University), where he perfected his English by watching television. For his sixteenth birthday he received from his father a leather-bound journal with an inscription: "Another notebook for the same game. Spontaneous self-expression must now turn into studied attempts at conciseness and discipline." He spent the rest of his life obeying that imperative, taking degrees at universities in Srinagar and Delhi, State College, Pennsylvania, and Tucson, Arizona, then teaching at writers' conferences and universities across America. In the classroom he was at once rigorous and droll: he could spot promising seeds in otherwise uninspired exercises; he liked to turn a poem inside out, reading it from the last line to the first, in search of its secret heart; he could not bear shoddy work. He once quipped that a bad line should be put up against a wall and shot—a joke that takes on weight when you consider that he was mindful of the number of people executed in the last century in precisely this fashion, for the relationship between art and politics was uppermost in his mind. And his playfulness served a larger purpose. When a student begged him to raise his grade, Shahid agreed, on the condition that he sing all the verses of "Achy Breaky Heart." Which the student did, in a cracking voice.

His own readings were a kind of stand-up tragedy, dark poems punctuated by hilarious asides. He would stop mid-poem to pose for a photograph, exclaiming, "I love to be photographed," or to castigate someone in the audience for daring to leave early. More than one embarrassed person returned to their seats after Shahid asked, "Are you leaving me? Don't leave me!" Once, when an overflowing crowd forced some to sit on the floor by the lectern, he crowed, "I love to have white people sitting at my feet!" What stayed with listeners, though, was the exquisite tension between his casual asides and the seriousness of his work. He was a darkly humorous poet who wanted to publish poems in journals beginning with all the letters of the alphabet; lacking a Z, he tried to convince the editor of ZYZZYVA, which published only writers living on the West Coast, that as a citizen of the Pacific Rim he belonged in its pages. His one reservation about becoming a contributing editor to *Tin House* was its name—he already had his *T.* Couldn't the publisher consider a name beginning with a *Z*?

One day at lunch in Venice, California, he gave me a copy of Xavier Villaurrutia's poems in translation, *Hieroglyphs of Desire*; inspired by the sleek women in bikinis rollerblading by, he wrote on the title page that here "we again learn, on the boardwalk, that some hieroglyphs of desire move on wheels." In a used bookstore in Syracuse, when he discovered a signed copy of his *Walk Through the Yellow Pages*, which he had presented to a married couple, he bought the chapbook and sent it back to them with instructions never to sell it again.

Shahid took seriously his role as godfather to our oldest daughter, Hannah, who was born during my first semester of teaching at the College of the Holy Cross in Worcester, Massachusetts, not far from his converted flat in Northampton's former jail. ("Jail" was one title he considered for the book of poems he published as *Rooms Are Never Finished*.) He brought gifts for her from the silver emporium in New Delhi, asked after her in every phone call, drove through the snow for her christening in Pennsylvania, colliding along the way with another car and denting his Nissan Stanza (chosen for its name, not its performance). After the service, Lisa asked him if as a Shiite Muslim he felt uncomfortable assenting to the tenets of Christianity.

"Not at all," he replied. "I take it all very metaphorically."

Which did not mean that he had a cavalier attitude toward religion. Incidents from Islamic history triggered his imagination, his poems were rich in references to the Koran (which in his last years inspired in him a kind of devotion), and his respect for religious ritual, in any denomination, was profound. Poetry was for him a form of prayer and petition to the gods of desire, who rewarded his unconditional faith with splendid works on love and the inevitability of loss.

When Hannah was little, I figured that as an adult she would realize how lucky she was to have Shahid in her life. But she seemed to grasp this even before the gravity of his illness dawned on her, around the time that I accepted a position at the University of Iowa. My in-laws moved with us to Iowa City (Lisa's father was also dying of brain cancer), and within weeks of our arrival Shahid came to recite his poems for the International Writing Program (IWP)—a memorable event in a city rich in literary history. He stayed with us through the weekend for Hannah's fifth birthday—which fell, providentially, on the day her grandfather died. A hospice chaplain led a memorial service around his deathbed (Shahid did not attend), making a graceful transition from praising Hannah's "Papa" to rejoicing in the happy prospect of her birthday party, which took place that afternoon at the skating rink. Shahid was there, and Lisa and her mother, and Hannah's friends from preschool. One parent asked me to take her infant daughter for a skate, and as I glided around the rink with her in my arms, my heart was breaking. In memory of Lisa's father, my staff gave us an apple tree. It did not survive the winter.

On the night before Shahid died, Hannah covered the walls of my study with her drawings, carefully taping pictures of houses and animals to every empty space, intuiting that in a dark time I needed the consolation of art. In the morning, after receiving the grim news from his brother, I took Hannah to the rink, and for forty-five minutes we skated hand in hand, as she sketched out in elaborate detail her next birthday party. We would need to get a trampoline, and dig a swimming pool in the backyard, and bake at least two cakes, because one of her friends had severe allergies. I waited until we were in the car driving home to tell her that Shahid was gone.

"I know," she said. In the rearview mirror I could see

that she was thinking. Then: "How long will it take for him to get to heaven? Faster than a car? A plane?"

"Even faster," I said.

"Good," she said. "Then I can talk to him, like I do with Papa."

I was surprised to hear that she spoke regularly with her late grandfather, and when I asked her what they talked about she replied, "He just wants to know if I'm happy."

Shahid would have approved, buoyancy being for him the best response to self-pity; as he wrote, "for whose world is not in ruins? whose?" When an Indian American student complained to him about feeling alienated from his classmates because he was different, Shahid laughed. "Of course you're different," he said. "Celebrate that difference." He fashioned a poetics out of difference, liberating himself from the shackles of staid thinking. Before his mother died, he liked to say that he refused to suffer for more than thirty seconds over anything. With her death, though, came a more complex vision of the human condition, which corresponded to his deepening engagement with English and Urdu literary traditions, politics, and religion.

Central to his poetic development was the friendship he struck up with my distant relation James Merrill. If the free-verse extravaganza of Shahid's first book, *The Half-Inch Himalayas*, had introduced an exotic mixture of wit, imagery, and historical awareness to American poetry, now under Merrill's sway he became a sophisticated formalist. In *A Nostalgist's Map of America*, *The Country without a Post Office*, and *Rooms Are Never Finished*, he wrote in a variety of forms, preferring syllabic to metrical verse because he could not hear stresses in English. The sound he created, an exuberant music that was slightly ahead of or behind the beat, swelled in a trio of canzones. This medieval Italian lyrical form, hendecasyllabic lines with a demanding rhyme scheme, is extremely difficult to write, and Shahid's prowess in the form prompted the poet Anthony Hecht to remark that he deserved a place in the *Guinness Book of World Records*. The third one, "The Veiled Suite," was completed the weekend after he learned that he had lost his battle with cancer. Its origins lay in a dream from the eve of his first biopsy, in which he was visited by a figure for Death: "'No mortal has or will ever lift my veil,' / he says. Strokes my arm. What poison is his eyes?" As he neared the end of the composition of his poem Shahid could not remember the beginning of each line he was working on—his assistant had to keep reading it back to him—and yet "The Veiled Suite" is completely coherent. It is also terrifying. How he accomplished this is a mystery as great as the last riveting lines: "I'm still alive, alive to learn from your eyes / that I am become your veil and I am all you see."

But for all the formal dexterity on display in his canzones Shahid will be remembered most for his efforts to bring the ghazal into English. "The ghazal," he liked to say, "is pronounced *ghuzzle*." And the average American poet's inability to say the word correctly upset him almost as much as the widespread belief that a ghazal could be written without obeying its formal imperatives. So he took it upon himself to properly introduce the form in lectures and essays on its history and virtues. He cajoled more than a hundred poets to write what he called "real ghazals in English" for an anthology, *Ravishing DisUnities*, inspiring yet more poets to try their hand at the form. Assigning exercises in writing ghazals became a staple of poetry workshops, and editors of literary journals who are inundated with ghazal submissions have Shahid to thank for reshaping our literary landscape, in the same way that in the sixteenth century the Italian sonnet's arrival in London irrevocably changed English poetry. Impossible to imagine Western literature without the sonnets of Wyatt,

Shakespeare, Donne, Milton, and others. Someday the same may be said of ghazals, beginning with Shahid's *Call Me Ishmael Tonight*, his posthumous homage to the poetic tradition of the country to which in his last decade he formally pledged allegiance, becoming an American citizen.

The ghazal dates back to seventh-century Arabia, coincides with Islam's rise, and figures in many literary traditions, including Farsi, Turkish, Urdu, Pashto, German, and Spanish. (Shahid loved García Lorca's ghazals.) It consists of a series of autonomous couplets, which may be comic, tragic, romantic, political, or religious in subject and tone, all lashed together by rhyme, refrain, and meter. In the opening couplet, the rhyme is repeated, establishing the scheme to which the poet, Shahid liked to say, becomes the slave. He translated Urdu's quantitative meters into syllabics, as in his best-known ghazal, which opens, "The only language of loss left in the world is Arabic— / These words were said to me in a language not Arabic." In its closing couplet, the *mukta* or signature couplet, the poet names him- or herself: "They ask me to tell them what *Shahid* means— / Listen: It means 'The Belovéd' in Persian, 'witness' in Arabic." These lines supplied the title for the Indian edition of his selected poems *The Beloved Witness*—and they were also inscribed on his gravestone.

Contrapuntal and *convergence* were two of his favorite words: his salacious wit stood in counterpoint to the puritanical thinking that in his view stifled American life, while literary and spiritual traditions from around the world converged in his work to create a new vision of our walk in the sun. He was a true cosmopolitan: that is, someone deeply rooted to a particular place—Kashmir—who felt at home wherever he found himself. He took pleasure in the number and range of places where we met, from Santa Fe to San Antonio to Seattle. I can hear him now, waking us in the morning, singing first a raga and then a song by Dire Straits. What he lacked in musicality—he could barely carry a tune—he made up for in enthusiasm.

In Shahid's last months he liked to listen to The Band's cover version of Bob Dylan's "I Shall Be Released." He would sit by the window in his brother's living room, the air swelling with music; only his family knew that he sang to take his mind off the pain. He was ever the courteous host, asking his steady stream of visitors if they had been served lunch or tea. Would they like to hear something different? Did they want to dance? The lyrics that never failed to make him weep—"I see my light come shining / From the west unto the east"—describe the trajectory of his life and work, a dazzling arc linking America and

Kashmir. He brightened our poetry by persuading us to write real ghazals in English—lights shining from the West unto the East.

Six months before Shahid died, a mutual friend suggested that we make a ghazal chain for him, to which nearly two hundred poets contributed couplets. The opening couplet has a curious history. I was in Maui taking care of Merwin's place, which Shahid and I facetiously referred to as the Promised Land, and one day, brewing a cup of tea during a long phone conversation with him and finding only honey to sweeten it, I intoned, "There is no sugar in the Promised Land." He seized on the poetic potential of my joke, and we laughed like madmen, playing around with lines to close the couplet. The refrain we came up with—"Swear by the olive in the God-kissed land"—was not a perfect rhyme, which pleased him all the more. (He once rhymed "Utah" with "blue tar," a rhyme that depended upon his Indian accent.) He insisted that we each write ghazals opening with this couplet, but to my regret I could not finish mine before he died. In his poem for me, "Land," which appears in *Call Me Ishmael Tonight*, he reverses the rhyme and refrain, reinforcing the idea that nothing is perfect, even in the Promised Land. He was always a realist. The ghazal chain for him closes with

his signature couplet: "At the moment the heart turns terrorist, / are Shahid's arms broken, O Promised Land?"

There was an ice storm the night before his funeral,
and in the morning the sunlight glittered off the icicles
hanging from the trees in the cemetery, where his family and friends gathered. The bearded imam recruited to
perform the burial service kept losing his place—a public display of incompetence that would have sent Shahid
into paroxysms of laughter. Adjacent to his grave was the
headstone of a World War II veteran. "Shahid's dream
has come true: to lie next to a man in uniform!" someone
quipped, bringing a note of levity to the occasion. After
the service there was a party at his brother's house, where
the mood darkened by the hour. At nightfall, driving back
to my hotel, I decided on a whim to visit Emily Dickinson's grave. Pennies and a sprig of holly had been left in
her honor, and it was consoling to think that Shahid's
future readers might one day travel to Northampton to do
the same for him.

Cornus officinalis, also known as Japanese cornel,
cornelian cherry, and medical dogwood, is used to treat
reproductive issues, liver problems, back pain, impotence,
and vertigo. But it cannot alleviate grief. For a long time
after Shahid died, I would reach for the phone to call him

whenever I heard a good joke or story, a reflexive gesture that day by day rekindled my grief; what surprised me was that the pain caused by his absence did not diminish. All the world was strange to me—"a foreign place," as Wang Wei wrote in his Double Nine poem—in which I was always "short one person." Eventually I finished the ghazal he had commanded me to write, invoking the root meaning of my name in the signature couplet, which offers a question in reply to his final question: "Will this Christ-bearer find his only friend / In the Promised Land—in blessèd Shahid's land?" Whatever the answer may be, I relish the light he bestowed upon my life. The dogwood berries and branches woven into my imagination have acquired color and texture with the passing of my poet-teachers and friends—Joseph Brodsky, William Matthews, Leslie Norris, Brewster Ghiselin, Mark Strand, Tomaž Šalamun, and, dearest of all, Shahid.

The Sound of Falling

The oleander was blossoming in the courtyard of the *tekija*, a Sufi dervish lodge carved into a cliff, and in the last light of a September afternoon the white blossoms shone against the red rock. More than forty species of birds nest in the cliff, which also houses the source of the Buna River, an emerald tributary of the Neretva flowing through Mostar, in southern Bosnia, where Sufi dervishes arrived in the fifteenth century. They flourished there until the Communist takeover of Yugoslavia in 1945, when they went underground; they resurfaced in 1991, when Yugoslavia began to break apart. Now there were seminarians talking in low tones at a table outside the kitchen, near a display of prayer ropes, shawls, kilims, and devotional books for sale. Our delegation from a literary festival in Sarajevo took seats at a picnic table, and a waiter brought cups of Turkish coffee and raki distilled from the fruit of the European dogwood (*Cornus mas*). In the gloaming we watched swallows sweep along the cliff.

I was thinking of Rumi, the thirteenth-century Sufi teacher regarded as the greatest mystical poet of Islam. Born in Afghanistan, he was just a boy when his family fled from advancing Mongol forces, first to Baghdad, then to Damascus, and finally to central Turkey. He married, started a family, and upon his father's death inherited his position as head of a madrassa. He studied sharia and Sufism, traveled to Damascus, preached and issued fatwas. One day he met a wandering dervish, Shams of Tabriz, who encouraged him to take up the ascetic life—an unsettling prospect for Rumi's family and followers. Shams had come to Anatolia in search of a mystical friendship, which suited Rumi's growing conviction that without grace a life devoted to the intellect can lead to spiritual aridity. He gave himself over to Shams, neglecting his students and family, and for three years they were closer than brothers until someone, perhaps his son, murdered the dervish. This tragedy inspired Rumi's poetic vocation: spinning in grief around a nail in the floor, he composed the first of thousands of ghazals in praise of his friend, ecstatic poems that teach his readers to seek divinity in every encounter, for union with the beloved is essential to progress in the spiritual life, the contours and textures of which Rumi devoted his remaining twenty-five years to illuminating. Poems came to him unbidden, and he likened himself to a reed, a vessel for the divine, which seemed to flow effortlessly through him. The nail in the floor around which he spun became the fixed point in the universe for the Mevlevi Order, or whirling dervishes, founded by his followers after his death—the men in long white robes and tall red hats, remembering God in the act of whirling and whirling, guided by the melodies of their master. The murmuring of their descendants here in the tekija brought to mind his poem on the nature of existence:

> Inside the Great Mystery that is,
> we don't really own anything.
> What is this competition we feel then,
> before we go, one at a time, through the same gate?

This was what I felt at our next destination—the ruins of East Mostar, the mainly Muslim side of the city, which in the war of shifting loyalties dividing the Bosnian Muslim, Croatian Catholic, and Serbian Orthodox communities had borne the brunt of destruction. The audience for our reading was small, and at the dinner afterward our host, a local Muslim journalist, apologized for failing to send out invitations. From the veranda of a restaurant overlooking the river we had a view of the temporary wooden bridge erected to replace the Old Bridge, Stari Most, a sixteenth-century Ottoman thing of wonder that had once linked the two sides of the city: a symbol of tolerance dynamited in the war. But the blocks of *tenelija* stone had been raised from the water. The bridge would be rebuilt.

Links between local Christians and Muslims would be harder to restore. The journalist, for example, blamed the West for the immorality sweeping the globe; homosexuality was his emblem of evil, and he wanted us to explain why the pope had sanctioned same-sex marriages. I could not disabuse him of his theological error, to say nothing of his intolerance, and I lacked Shahid's rapier wit, which he would have wielded to dissect my interlocutor.

"Too much tolerance leads to chaos," the Bosnian hissed.

This idea haunted me on my flight home the next day. September 10, 2001. My cell phone did not work in Bosnia, and without access to my e-mail I did not learn until we landed in Chicago that for three days in a row a Burmese writer in the IWP had been rushed to the hospital in a drunken stupor. This crisis took my mind off the Bosnian's venomous rant—which nonetheless came back to me days later, in the wake of the attacks on the World Trade Center and the Pentagon, when the father of one hijacker, insisting his son had nothing to do with the crime, used precisely the same language in an interview to castigate the "immoral" West. For this is the language of fundamentalists everywhere, of those who are uneasy with the changing mores of modernity—the advance of human rights for women and minorities ethnic, religious, and sexual; the rise of the information age; the effects of globalization. But the sense of dislocation common to members of the Islamic terrorist cells that a U.S.-led alliance would soon wage war against was little different from the shock felt by most Americans on 9/11.

That morning, one year into my tenure at the helm of the IWP, I was on the phone with a university lawyer discussing the plight of our Burmese writer. A judicial order to commit him to the psychiatric ward for detoxification had been signed, and I was asking about the legal ramifications for my program when she interrupted me.

"Oh my God," she said. "Turn on your TV."

Plumes of smoke were rising from one of the Twin Towers in New York City, and within moments flames erupted in the other building from the impact of a second hijacked airplane. My conversation with the lawyer ended before a television commentator said, "It is completely impossible to understand why this is happening and to figure out what in the world is going on," marking the advent of a new era in American history—which pundits, politicians, and policy makers would attempt to define even before I had escorted the Burmese writer from the hospital to his hotel to pack for his flight home. (Mindful that he had left one of the most repressive regimes in the world to spend most of his time in Iowa locked up in a psychiatric ward, I suggested to him that at least he had something to write about. He gave me a wan smile.)

The rest of that fateful day I spent in meetings with public safety officials and our foreign writers in residence, some of whom appeared happy to see America get its comeuppance. I could not wait to get home. Lisa had given birth to our second daughter, Abby, nine months before, and my fear for her and her sister was as nothing I had ever known. Their safety in the aftermath of 9/11, and Shahid's impending death, weighed on me, and I would spend the fall reflecting on the ways in which pain can lock up emotions—the subject of Emily Dickinson's famous meditation on loss, composed in 1862, the year of the greatest carnage in the Civil War:

After great pain, a formal feeling comes -
The Nerves sit ceremonious, like Tombs -
The stiff Heart questions 'was it He, that bore,'
And 'Yesterday, or Centuries before'?

The Feet, mechanical, go round -
A Wooden way
Of Ground, or Air, or Ought -
Regardless grown,
A Quartz contentment, like a stone -

This is the Hour of Lead -
Remembered, if outlived,
As Freezing persons, recollect the Snow -
First - Chill - then Stupor - then the letting go -

Dickinson's poems, almost half of which date from the Civil War, provide a map to the broken heart of a solitary woman—and of her country. All was torn asunder by the Confederate secession, a public betrayal that perhaps echoed events in Dickinson's affective life. Yet she found "a formal feeling" for her grief that transcended its private origin. In 1862, the pivotal year of the war, she vividly described the pain that Americans would feel again after 9/11. At the Battle of Antietam, more Americans were killed on our native soil than at any other time in our history. While neither side could claim victory at Antietam, Confederate general Robert E. Lee was forced to abandon his Maryland campaign, and his retreat prompted Abraham Lincoln to issue his Emancipation Proclamation, freeing the slaves.

The year 1862 marked another emancipation: Dickinson completed, on average, a poem a day—hers was a "Soul at the White Heat," which traced, among other things, the hour of lead that once again fell over this land on 9/11. Many hearts in this country, mine included, were stiffened by the treachery of the hijackers recruited to start a war with America. The days grew shorter, the leaves on the oaks in our backyard turned yellow and fell, and it occurred to me that if I did not transfigure my grief, private and public, into poetry I might end up as embittered as the journalist in Mostar. Dickinson's genius was to recognize how trauma can freeze emotions, sometimes permanently, and I knew that in the years to come, as I recollected the ash that fell like snow one September morning in New York City, my well-being, and that of my compatriots, would depend not only on luck, timing, and circumstances but on decisions made, individually and collectively, in the service of this new order. Who can say why some will waken from their frozen stupor, while others fall deeper into sleep?

The ash was still falling in November when I visited Ground Zero. The wooden walkway some climbed to peer into the wreckage was slippery with soot; the stench of death hung in the cold air. Men and women wept. Sidewalk vendors hawked American flags, T-shirts proclaiming *Never Forget*, and hats emblazoned with FDNY and NYPD insignia. A young woman embraced a policeman. I circled the site, conscious of what was missing—and of how absence may be described through what is there: the skeletal remains of a building, a makeshift shrine of plastic flowers and teddy bears, a chamber orchestra rehearsing in a church in which the pews are covered with plastic sheets. The mind reels in the face of such destruction—one reason why so many people turned to poetry in the days and weeks following 9/11. For poetry, as Robert Frost said, "is a momentary stay against confusion."

From Ground Zero I drove to Northampton to see Shahid for the last time. For three days we laughed and danced, ate and drank, retelling stories about our exotic meetings; when I returned three weeks later for his memorial service I clung to the memory of his buoyancy in the face of death. "The Leaves unhooked themselves from

Trees / And started all abroad," Dickinson wrote. These lines ran through my mind on my flight to Prague the day after his burial, providing a figure for the paper and ash that fell from the sky on 9/11—and for the grief I felt, both for myself and for my country. I recalled that as a teenager Dickinson had pressed flowers between the pages of her herbarium, which had more than four hundred specimens, including dogwoods—flowering, round-leaved, and alternate-leaved: the tree, I decided somewhere over the Atlantic, under which I hoped to be buried.

Meetings in Prague and then Bratislava kept me occupied until the weekend, when at last I had a chance to reflect on the losses of the autumn. I was staying in a castle, in a wine region near Bratislava, where a conference titled "Back in Europe" was concluding. Writers from Austria, Bulgaria, Croatia, Germany, and the former Yugoslavia had gathered to discuss their declining spiritual and material conditions. The spread of American culture was roundly condemned; the writings of Danielle Steel came in for particular scorn. The conference, convened by the Austrian Embassy, hearkened back to the Habsburg era, and it set me to wondering about the passing of old orders—the Dual Monarchy, National Socialism, Communism, perhaps even the American order. Here was a decisive moment in history: never had a country amassed so much power and wealth as America, and never had it seemed as easy to topple the edifice as in the first days and weeks after 9/11.

The feeling here, too, was of loss. No one could tell me the fate of the castle's Hungarian owners, who had collaborated with the Nazis. The castle belonged to the Slovak Literary Fund, explained a poet who had lost most of his family at Auschwitz; his latest book included a sequence about an angel with feathers blackened by the soot of the crematoria. And my host, whose father had just died, kept bursting into tears. We had met in Prague, where he gave a reading that drew from his Czech audience questions tinged with nostalgia: Isn't it a pity that Czechs and Slovaks are so distant now? There was even talk of requiring visas to travel between the two countries, which for much of the last century had been united. But now the Czech Republic was ensconced in the West. Slovakia was caught in a geopolitical netherworld.

The first night I slept in the Black Room, where Nikita Khrushchev, Mikhail Gorbachev, and Václav Havel had stayed. In the morning, when the other writers departed, my host showed me to a smaller room by a balcony (from which someone had leapt to his death), and then took his leave. It sounds romantic—a weekend alone in an empty castle—but soon I fell into despair. The walls of the salon were lined with paintings of dead writers; the glass bookcases containing their works were locked. A wedding party arrived—the bride and groom, a photographer, and the driver of a black Mercedes with a doll in a white dress propped on the hood. The photographer snapped the couple's picture on the front steps. When they tried to drive off, the car stalled.

It was the coldest winter in a century; a foot of snow lay on the ground; the poplar-lined driveway to the castle had not been cleared. The restaurant in the neighboring village was closed, as was the café. A pair of death notices was taped to the wall of the municipal building, which doubled as the bus station. At the top of a hill a cross-country skier was breaking a trail in a field, a lone figure set against the overcast sky. Villagers roamed in the park surrounding the castle, picked pine boughs, pulled children on sleds. I walked through woods thick with mistletoe to a shrine marking the spot where the Virgin Mary supposedly had appeared. Snow crunched underfoot; a jay followed me from tree to tree, squawking. I had never felt such desolation.

Back in the castle I took tea in an alcove above the

reception area, between a statue of the Madonna and Child and a large white oven decorated with pink flowers. The light was fading in the trees. Two older women, the weekend manager and the cook, were talking by the front door; their cigarette smoke wafted up the circular staircase. My thoughts turned to the recent discovery of a novel by the Hungarian writer Sándor Márai, *Embers*, published in 1942. When Márai fled to the West in 1948, the Communist authorities burned his work, and when he committed suicide in San Diego in 1989, just before the Berlin Wall came down, he was virtually unknown. But new editions of his books, translated into more than twenty languages, were earning him a place in world literature. Knopf planned to translate into English and publish his entire body of work.

Embers is set in a castle in 1941, in the Hungarian forest. The war is a distant presence for a retired general, who over the course of a single night tells the story of the day at the turn of the century when his world collapsed. He and his best friend, faithful members of the emperor's army, went hunting early that morning; when a deer emerged in a clearing ahead of them, the general made a terrible discovery. "And then something happened that I could never prove in a court of law," the general explains to his friend, who after forty-one years has crossed mine-laden seas to visit him, "but that I can tell you because you know it already—"

it was a little thing, I felt you move, more clearly than if I'd been watching you. You were close behind me, and a fraction to the side. I felt you raise your gun, set it on your shoulder, take aim, and close one eye. I felt the gun slowly swivel. My head and the deer's head were in the exact same line of fire, and at the exact same height; at most there may have been four inches between the two targets. I felt your hand tremble, and I knew as surely as only the hunter can assess a particular situation in the woods, that from where you were standing you could not be taking aim at the deer. Please understand me: it was the hunting aspect, not the human, that held my attention right then. I was, after all, a devotee of hunting, with some expertise in its technical problems, such as the angle at which one must position oneself in relation to a deer standing unsuspecting at a distance of three hundred paces. Given the geometrical arrangement of the marksman and the two targets, the whole thing was quite clear, and I could calculate what was going on in the mind of the person behind my back. You took aim for half a minute, and I knew that down to the second, without a watch. I knew you were not a fine shot and that all I had to do was move my head a fraction and the bullet would whistle past my ear and maybe hit the deer. I knew that one movement would suffice and the bullet would remain in the barrel of your gun. But I also knew I couldn't move because my fate was no longer mine to control: some moment had come, something was going to happen of its own volition. And I stood there, waiting for the shot, waiting for you to pull the trigger and put a bullet through the head of your friend. It was a perfect situation: no witnesses, the gamekeeper and the dogs were a long way back, it was one of those well-known "tragic accidents" that are detailed every year in the newspapers. The half minute passed and still there was no shot. Suddenly the deer smelled danger and exploded into motion with a single bound that took him out of our sight to safety in the undergrowth. We still didn't move. And then, very slowly, you let the gun sink.

The general's discovery that his wife and best friend have been conspiring against him, a betrayal played out in silence, changes everything. His friend leaves for the tropics, and the general moves into the hunting lodge adjacent to the castle, refusing to speak to his wife again, even when she falls sick and dies. The rest of his days he devotes to rehearsing the story of that day, which he will tell his friend, if he ever gets the chance. Indeed his life depends upon him telling this story well, in order to elicit from his listener answers to the questions he has carried with him ever since the day his life fell apart.

Embers may be read as an allegory about the demise of various orders—a family, a friendship, the aristocracy, the Concert of Europe, the Dual Monarchy. Nor is it an accident that it is set in the midst of world war, when another global order was taking shape—an order that disappeared within months of Márai's death. Now his book was finding an audience even as another order was being created. The general takes revenge by recounting his betrayal, spinning a tale at once haunting and true. Others will seek revenge in a different form. Endings may be quiet and remote: a shot not fired in the woods, the silent unraveling of a marriage, a friendship abandoned without explanation. Or they may be as thunderous as a plane slicing into a building, a bomb exploding in a market. Writers are in the business of recording endings, each with its own music. And there is pleasure in getting it right, as the general learns when his guest departs at daybreak. His old nurse asks if he feels calmer. Yes, he replies. As they walk through the portrait gallery he instructs her to restore his wife's picture to its place on the wall, for she can no longer hurt him. The nurse makes the sign of the cross on his forehead, and then they kiss.

"But like every kiss," Márai confides, "this one is an answer, a clumsy but tender answer to a question that eludes the power of language." A kind of absolution is thus conferred upon the teller of this tale—and upon the reader, too. Who can resist that?

Black Watch

In November 2004, on the eve of the American presidential election, three Scottish soldiers from the Black Watch regiment and their Iraqi interpreter were killed in a blast from a suicide car bomb near Camp Dogwood, fifty kilometers south of Baghdad. The tragedy inspired the National Theatre of Scotland to commission Gregory Burke's award-winning verbatim play *Black Watch*, which explores the consequences of the U.S.-led invasion and occupation of Iraq. With a skillful mix of stories collected from veterans of Scotland's famed regiment, song, dance, and video sequences, the play raises questions about the nature of our involvement in Iraq—and the costs of sending armed forces on an ill-defined mission. "So what was it then?" a soldier wonders. His question, which concerns not only the fatal attack but the nature of the country unraveling before their eyes, begs other questions: Why was the Bush administration hell-bent on going to war? How to account for their failure to plan for a lengthy occupation? What made them think they could spread democracy across the Middle East at the barrel of a gun?

Articulating such questions can wake us from our stupor, clear our vision, and heal the soul sickness brought on by the war on terror—which accounts for the play's success when it debuted at the Edinburgh Festival Fringe in 2006. Its revelation of the forms of paralysis—physical, moral, political—that terror can induce captivated audiences in Scotland and then New York and Los Angeles, for in the crude expressions of men ordered into an impossible situation Burke discovered a language and a music adequate to the experience of war.

The action alternates between a pool hall in Fife, where surviving members of the Black Watch regiment recount their experiences to a journalist, and Camp Dogwood in Iraq, where from the moment of their arrival they combat heat, sandstorms, scorpions, boredom, bad food and water, and shelling. "You'd think they would have fucking let us get unpacked before they attacked us," one soldier mutters. "Cheeky bastards," replies another.

"My darling, you said in my last email I sounded worried," an officer reads aloud from a message home. "Well, we are here in Dogwood and the task does look quite challenging." While an armored battalion takes up blocking positions in the desert southwest of Fallujah, his men must cut off the insurgents' lines of communication and prevent terrorists from reaching Baghdad. "Our orders," he explains, "are to apply our own tactics and, in contrast to the 'firepower and force protection first' style of the Americans, get out among the local population and win hearts and minds." His government, he adds, may not appreciate the risks of mounting such a mission among insurgents who may have already mapped the battalion's positions, with potentially deadly consequences.

Mixing with locals was a tactic adopted by some American military units. The bungled occupation of Iraq, which triggered a civil war, amplifying the global condemnation of American foreign policy, convinced a handful of military leaders to engage civilians on a personal level, in hopes of winning hearts and minds—a cornerstone of cultural diplomacy, which is defined by Milton C. Cummings as "the exchange of ideas, information, art, and other aspects of culture among nations and their people in order to foster mutual understanding." The term was not in my lexicon when I was hired to direct the IWP, which from its origins in 1967 has received funding from the U.S. State Department. And I did not give it much thought until 2004, when I was appointed to a State Department advisory committee on cultural diplomacy; our mandate from Congress was to research and devise strategies to dowse the flames of anti-Americanism fanned by the war in Iraq. On a fact-finding mission to Muscat, Cairo, and London, my colleagues assigned me the task of writing our report on the subject. Thus began my education in international relations. In the coming years I would log more than a million miles on cultural diplomacy missions for the State Department to countries of strategic interest, including Afghanistan, Iraq, Iran, Lebanon, Libya, Syria, Sudan and South Sudan, Israel and Palestine, Uzbekistan, Turkmenistan, Haiti, Cuba, Bolivia, Venezuela, the Congo, Zimbabwe . . . My whereabouts were a running joke with my friends (some thought I worked for the CIA), my passport thickened with supplemental pages, and I learned that connecting with others—fielding questions in a Somali refugee camp, lecturing at universities in Baghdad, meeting with minority Chinese writers in Kunming—thrilled me.

It was usually on the flight home from some far-flung place that I would be overcome with misgivings about the usefulness of cultural diplomacy and the morality of working for an administration guilty of hubris—for defying the international community to launch a war in violation of the UN Charter; for staggering incompetence in its occupation of Iraq; and for the war crimes of torturing enemy combatants. William Merwin's counsel to maintain my independence echoed in my memory as an indictment; whatever rationale I mustered to justify my travels—the value of presenting another vision of America to the world, the search for writing material, the need to provide for my family—rang hollow in my ears. Midflight, numb from watching movies, I would judge my so-called diplomatic skills—an instinct to forge consensus, to compromise—to be proof only of moral cowardice. My exhaustion upon arrival and in the following weeks at home owed little to jet lag.

One stage direction reads: "*There is a blast outside the wagon.*" In the performance I attended, at UCLA's Freud Playhouse, the wagon was a hollowed-out pool table crammed with five soldiers in combat gear. When the sound of an explosion shook the auditorium, the soldiers tumbled into one another, orders were shouted, the wagon lurched from side to side, and confusion reigned until a soldier described their predicament.

"We've been hit. We're going nowhere."

A fitting description of post-9/11 America. And this

play, about the costs of reassigning the Black Watch regiment from a safe outpost in Basra to Camp Dogwood to support American forces, was a symbol of the new order created by Al Qaeda; it was also a piece of theater diplomacy, sponsored by the British Council, that for American audiences illuminated some unintended consequences of our Mesopotamian adventure. Drama can clarify a crisis—personal and political, religious and social—and in its attention to the textures of daily life for soldiers in the war zone *Black Watch* brought into focus my misgivings about the hell to which we had consigned hundreds of thousands of troops, and millions of Iraqis. Here was a way to confront our collective responsibility for all the bloodshed: a necessary corrective to the narrative taking hold of an arrogant nation acting recklessly. For my research on cultural diplomacy made clear that our refusal to acknowledge the costs, scale, and meaning of the Iraq debacle not only diminished American standing around the world but also hindered the ability of lawmakers to formulate effective policies. How to deal with the harm done in our name? *Black Watch* offered a model for reckoning with other crises born of the war on terror—the prison scandals at Abu Ghraib, Bagram, and Guantánamo; the "extraordinary rendition" of terrorist suspects; the Justice Department memoranda condoning torture, which gave license to violators of the Geneva Conventions. These crimes demanded an accounting, which was not forthcoming. Absent judicial review, journalists and nongovernmental organizations took up the challenge of tracing the path that had led us astray. The information they unearthed led the Senate to investigate the CIA's detention and interrogation program; the publication of its findings would reveal the true horror of what had been done on our behalf.

Black Watch also prompted a reconsideration of the journalist's role in ferreting out the truth, at home and abroad. When the writer asks what it felt like to be attacked, for example, one veteran, Stewarty, grows agitated. It turns out that when the suicide car bomber detonated his payload, Stewarty broke his arm. Now he circles the writer in a menacing dance, reenacting his response to the injury, which was to rebreak his arm again and again to avoid returning to duty.

> It would get better and I would break it myself.
>
> *Beat*
>
> Get better. Break it myself.
>
> *Beat*
>
> Better. Break it.

> *Beat*
>
> Better.
>
> *Beat*
>
> Break it. (*Pause.*) Write that down.
>
> **Writer** I will.
>
> **Stewarty** Write it down way a broken arm though.
>
> *Stewarty grabs the Writer's arm.*

This turn of phrase brings to mind former secretary of state Colin Powell's Pottery Barn analogy: if you break it, he warned Bush before the invasion, you own it. This is reflected in the language itself. Just as the military breaks individuals down in order to meld them into a cohesive fighting unit, so does the playwright break apart the language, laying bare its violent underpinnings. The vocabulary of *Black Watch* is at once brutal and restricted, as it often is in war. In *The Things They Carried*, the definitive work of fiction about the Vietnam War, Tim O'Brien advises mothers not to send their sons to war if they do not want to hear them curse. But what poetry we hear in the timing of the soldiers' jokes, in their quick rejoinders, in the power of their cursing. There is poetry in common speech, which is all these soldiers have, along with occasional flashes of insight and the curse of memory.

The scene raises another issue: We know that soldiers wound themselves to get out of the fray. We know they may experience survivor's guilt upon their return to civilian life. But we cannot know what they went through in the war—which is what sends Stewarty over the edge. He wants to break the writer's arm so that he will know what it is like to be attacked. His is the question that only literature can answer: How to know something that we have not experienced? *Black Watch* bridges the gap between what we know and what we do not know.

When I first went to Sarajevo to cover the siege, another journalist told me that what makes the evening news is the worst of what occurs in a war zone, but in the Bosnian capital what you saw on television was what you experienced every day. I learned that what might be crystallized in a dispatch from Sniper Alley, or narrated in a radio report with gunfire crackling in the background, or filmed at night with tracer rounds fired from the surrounding hills, was as nothing compared to the daily lives of men, women, and children trying to survive—and trying to discover some meaning in the hell they found themselves in.

Cultural diplomacy was one way to make amends, and the missions I undertook, fueled by guilt and wanderlust, were in the service of Winston Churchill's belief that "it is better to jaw-jaw than to war-war." For in nearly every encounter I had, even in the most inhospitable circumstances, where political differences loomed large, it was possible to find common ground on which to build a measure of trust. This I kept in mind on a mission to Baghdad in 2012, flying at dusk on a State Department Embassy Air Dash-8, seated by a woman with a blonde ponytail, a defense contractor who promptly fell asleep. I was gazing out the window at the rooftops in a desert town, trying to imagine the daily routines of the people living there, when suddenly there was a flash of light, an explosion, a wave of heat washing over the cabin.

"Oh, shit!" cried the woman, waking wild-eyed.

To my surprise the plane kept flying—the thought passed through my mind that I might be in the afterlife—and long seconds ticked by before another contractor spoke from across the aisle: "Flares, maybe." A minute passed, and then the pilot confirmed over the intercom that decoy flares had automatically deployed as a countermeasure to a shot fired from below. He hoped there would not be another one, and indeed we landed thirty minutes later without incident. But the sound of detonating flares would ring in my ears for a long time.

On a separate mission to Basra, in southern Iraq, confined for security reasons to the base from which the Black Watch had been ordered to move to Camp Dogwood, I reread Burke's play, in the last scene of which an officer addresses a soldier:

It takes three hundred years to build an army that's admired and respected around the world. But it only takes three years pissing about in the desert in the biggest western foreign policy disaster ever to fuck it up completely.

Beat.

But you didn't hear that from me.

Beat.

We could be off to Afghanistan next. It's going to be exactly the same. Kandahar. Helmand province. It's the only place on the planet that might be slightly more dangerous than here.

The noise of an explosion.

We're going to be hearing that noise for years to come.

His verdict on the reputation of the Black Watch also applied to American foreign policy. And when the play ends with the troops declaring that they joined the army not for the government, British or Scottish, but for their regiment, their company, their platoon, their section, and, most decisively, their mates, we not only feel the power of the bonds forged by war but we wonder why this camaraderie was exploited for such ignoble purposes.

"That's what a regiment is," a soldier says. "It's history."

It is no accident that the Black Watch history narrated earlier in the play in a mesmerizing fashion—a soldier spirited around the stage, changing uniforms as he recites the different battles fought by his regiment—concludes in Mesopotamia. "Here we are. Again." For history does repeat itself, tragically or farcically, fulfilling a design that remains incomprehensible.

Dogwood Diplomacy

Dogwood diplomacy was the nickname bestowed upon a State Department initiative to promote friendship with Japan, celebrating a small but symbolic event in the history of relations between the two countries. In 1912, during the Taft administration, the mayor of Tokyo sent three thousand cherry trees to Washington, D.C., a gift that each spring draws more than a million visitors to the capital to see the trees in blossom. After Taft left office, his wife sent a handful of dogwoods to be planted in Tokyo, and in 1982 American schoolchildren collected a million dogwood seeds to exchange for a million cherry seeds collected by Japanese schoolchildren. Yet the Tokyo mayor's gift was not formally reciprocated until 2012, when Secretary of State Hillary Clinton marked its hundredth anniversary, during a state visit by Japanese prime minister Yoshihiko Noda, with the announcement that the U.S. government would deliver three thousand native dogwood seedlings to Japan.

The gift of trees, chosen specially for the soil and climate of the island nation, was intended to reinforce the goodwill generated by the Obama administration's decision to sharply reduce the number of U.S. Marines stationed on Okinawa—a point of contention for Okinawans tired of the noise, crime, and environmental degradation associated with the continuing American military presence long after the end of the war—and by the administration's support for the victims of the March 2011 Tōhoku earthquake, tsunami, and nuclear disaster at the Fukushima power plant. Dogwoods thus played a role in the diplomacy shaping the administration's strategic pivot from the Middle East to Asia, a policy shift made in recognition of China's rising economic and military power.

"Rarely has a country grown in such dramatic fashion strategically as China has," a State Department official explained at a 2011 Foreign Policy Initiative forum on the pivot to Asia, "probably even more dramatic than the arrival of the United States in the 1890s and the 1920s." American anxiety over the economic power of China, which at the time held more than a trillion dollars in U.S. Treasury bills, notes, and bonds, was exacerbated by its

buildup of armed forces, disputes with Japan over the uninhabited Senkaku Islands, and land-reclamation projects
to extend its territorial claims in the South China Sea, a
vital shipping corridor rich in natural gas and oil reserves.
China's challenge to the system of maritime trade and
commerce established by the United States after World
War II alarmed Japan and other countries in the region.
Hence the Obama administration's decision to rebalance
its strategic interests.

It fell to Richard Olsen, a research geneticist at the
National Arboretum in Washington, to organize the lo-
gistics of this diplomatic initiative, first gathering flowering dogwoods from across the country, including half a
dozen rare varieties prized by Japanese nurserymen, then
coordinating their shipment overseas. State Department
priorities—to send full-grown trees in leaf, during the
growing season, before Clinton left office—overrode best
horticultural practices, and after a significant portion
of the first batch of trees delivered on cargo planes died
(coincidentally, the first cherry trees sent to Washington
succumbed to disease and insect infestation, inspiring
legislation to quarantine plants arriving from abroad), it
was decided that henceforth bare-root dogwoods would
be shipped in winter, maintained by a Japanese grower

through the summer, and then planted around the country in autumn ceremonies.

Olsen relished tracking down rare varieties that might thrive in Japan. He had extensive contacts in the trade and at botanical gardens, one of whom inevitably would know, say, a retired nurseryman in Tennessee who could collect the necessary bud sticks for grafting.

"That's the great thing about the nursery industry," he told me over the phone. "People will move heaven and earth to get you some bud wood" for propagation.

Okinawa's tropical climate presented a challenge separate from the political complications arising from the continuing U.S. military presence. "Our temperate trees need to experience cold," he explained, "which acts as a trigger to let them know when spring is truly here. They have to sense that they've been through a winter. When things start to warm up, if they've experienced enough of what we call chill hours, near or below freezing, they'll leaf out." Thus if a flowering dogwood adapted to conditions in upstate New York needs two thousand chilling hours before it can leaf out, it cannot be transplanted successfully in Georgia. Olsen was therefore working with nurserymen throughout the South to locate a certain cultivar named Bobby, discovered long ago in Louisiana, which might do well in Okinawa. Although no one knew where to find it anymore, Olsen had not given up hope.

"These dogwoods are rare," he said. "They're worth cultivating. I want them for our collection. If we can conserve them and share them, that's the best of both worlds. That's what keeps me excited, regardless of the politics or anything else."

Ideally, the dogwoods, planted over several years, in Tokyo and Okinawa and memorial gardens under construction in Fukushima, would be the spark to rekindle collaboration among American and Japanese foundations, educational institutions, and individuals. Cultural diplomacy would not erase the legacy of ill will between the two countries, created on one hand by Japan's sneak attack on Pearl Harbor, the Bataan Death March, and other atrocities, and on the other by the American firebombing of Tokyo and dropping of atomic bombs on Hiroshima and Nagasaki. In the face of China's arrival on the world stage, however, the gift of dogwoods—a symbol of durability in the West, of reciprocity and gift giving in the East—might win hearts and minds in Japan, in the same way that those familiar with the provenance of the cherry trees in Washington might take a kinder view of their former enemy.

I had no inkling of this connection when I first saw the cherry trees, on my confirmation-class trip to the capital. All I knew at thirteen was that I loathed the Episcopal priest chaperoning us, a vindictive man who kicked misbehaving boys with a thick steel boot (a childhood bout of polio had left one leg shorter than the other), and from the time we checked into a hostel near the National Cathedral I plotted against him. When I saw him talking to another priest in the parking lot, two floors below, a plan took shape: I would hurl a banana at him, a friend would pull the blind down to hide my face, and vengeance would be ours. In the event my aim was perfect, the banana hitting him square in the jaw, but my friend was laughing so hard that he let go of the blind, betraying my position. The priest bellowed that I would pay for this.

At breakfast the next morning he informed me that my punishment was to eat the banana, which, fortunately, my friend retrieved from the parking lot and disposed of before the priest could make good on his threat.

The first stop for our class was a tour of the Capitol building, of which I remember nothing except the priest telling us that we would walk to the Washington Monument, a mile away. Because it was a fine spring morning, four of us decided to make a run for it, ignoring the shouts of the priest hobbling through the National Mall, lagging far behind. He was just a figure in the distance by the time we stopped to rest under a cherry tree. Blossoms were falling in the wind as we debated what to do if he got violent. A black boy named John Paul Jones, who had played the role of Fagan in our confirmation-class production of *Oliver Twist*, sipping the dregs of the liquor bottles on the bar shelves in the last act, said he had an uncle living in town: if worse came to worst, we could stay with him. When the priest arrived, winded and angry, it took him a minute to catch his breath and even longer to light his pipe in the wind, match after match.

Finally he spoke. "If you disobey me again, I'll put you in the custody of the District of Columbia police."

John Paul Jones chortled. "My uncle can bail us out," he said. "Then we'll get drunk at his place." Before the shocked priest could reply, we lit out for the monument, ran up and down all 897 steps twice, each time counting them aloud, and then collapsed on the grass. The priest was nowhere to be seen. It dawned on me that there was no longer any reason to fear him: however hard he kicked, whatever he might say to the police or our parents, he could not hurt us. What a marvelous thing it was to discover that he had no real power over us.

This revelation chimed with my sense that the myth of George Washington refusing to lie when asked if he had cut down his father's favorite cherry tree was bunkum. How to explain its persistence? Belief is integral to the human condition, and Americans in their new republic hungered to believe in their first president's trustworthiness; hence the myth of the cherry tree, which did not appear until the fifth edition of Parson Weems's best-selling biography, in 1806, seven years after Washington's death. Weems, a bookseller and itinerant preacher, knew his readers were avid for information about the father of their country—"that illustrious man," he wrote, "and Christian hero"—so he borrowed an English folktale to illustrate Washington's lifelong probity. Thirty years later, this myth was incorporated into the McGuffey's Readers schoolbooks, which in the next century sold more than 120 million copies—one reason why the virtues of truth telling were extolled in my childhood through an apocryphal story. "The real history of consciousness starts with one's first lie," wrote the Russian poet Joseph Brodsky, which in his case meant feigning ignorance of his Jewish identity when filling out an application for membership to his school library. For me, it was nodding assent to a teacher in grade school repeating a story that I knew in my heart had to be untrue: no six-year-old armed with a hatchet would say, "Father, I cannot tell a lie."

Washington's diaries and letters are a more reliable gauge of his character. "Within a week of his taking command of the Continental Army at Cambridge, Massachusetts, in July 1775," notes the editor of his papers, Philander D. Chase, "Washington began a regular correspondence with his distant cousin Lund Washington, who served as manager of Mount Vernon during the war." In August 1776, for example, one month after the adoption of the Declaration of Independence and with the Battle of Long Island about to start, he took time out from preparing for the largest military engagement of the Revolutionary War to write at some length to Lund, detailing what trees to plant and where around the mansion, to which northern and southern wings were being added:

> I mean to have groves of Trees at each end of the dwelling House, that at the South end to range in a line from the South East Corner to Colo. Fairfax's, extending as low as another line from the Stable to the dry well, and towards the Coach House, Hen House, & Smoak House as far as it can go for a Lane to be left for Carriages to pass to, & from the Stable and Wharf. from the No. Et Corner of the

other end of the House to range so as to Shew the Barn
&ca. in the Neck—from the point where the old Barn used
to Stand to the No. Et Corner of the Smiths Shop, & from
thence to the Servants Hall, leaving a passage between the
Quarter & Shop, and so East of the Spinning & Weaving
House (as they used to be called) up to a Wood pile, & so
into the yard between the Servts Hall & the House newly
erected—these Trees to be Planted without any order or
regularity (but pretty thick, as they can at any time be
thin'd) and to consist that at the North end, of locusts
altogether. & that at the South, of all the clever kind of
Trees (especially flowering ones) that can be got, such as
Crab apple, Poplar, Dogwood, Sasafras, Lawrel, Willow
(especially yellow & Weeping Willow, twigs of which may
be got from Philadelphia) and many others which I do not
recollect at present—these to be interspersed here and
there with ever greens such as Holly, Pine, and Cedar, also
Ivy—to these may be added the Wild flowering Shrubs
of the larger kind, such as the fringe Tree & several other
kinds that might be mentioned.

The particularity of his instructions is striking, especially on the eve of what he knew would be a difficult,
if not impossible, battle for control of New York City.

Washington's forces were outnumbered, outgunned, in-experienced, and disorganized. (In Brooklyn, livid at the sight of carts and horses driving every which way and soldiers haphazardly firing their guns, he wrote to their commanding officer, "The distinction between a well regulated army and a mob is the good order and discipline of the first, and the licentious and disorderly behavior of the latter.") In addition, as David McCullough explains in *1776*, a history of that pivotal year, "There was more sickness in the ranks than at any time before. Only a few of his officers had ever faced an enemy on the field of battle. He himself had never commanded an army in battle." Worse, Washington divided his forces in the Battle of Long Island, in expectation of a frontal attack—which did not begin until ten thousand British soldiers secretly marched through an unguarded pass to turn the American flank. The Continental Army was routed, with three hundred men killed and more than a thousand captured, some to be run through with bayonets, others starved in prison ships anchored in New York Harbor. Washington organized the stealthy evacuation of his army, crossing the East River in the dead of night without the loss of a single life, a daring move that won the admiration of his foes and his compatriots' dismay—the first of several retreats that fall. Henceforth he would fight a defensive war, delaying his return to Mount Vernon for seven years, during which he corresponded regularly with Lund, along with generals, congressmen, governors, local committees, militia officers, and private citizens. Chase argues that Washington's "letters were more important than shot and shell in winning his most important battles: the fight to preserve his army and make it an effective fighting force, and the fight to convince his diverse fellow citizens to lay aside their differences and rally to the support of the American cause." His war of words laid the groundwork for success on the battlefield.

But for now this seemed far-fetched. Two weeks after the Long Island debacle, with British forces shelling Manhattan and Hessians executing American prisoners in Brooklyn, Washington rode into battle on a cornfield in Manhattan's Murray Hill, where his men were in a panic. Enraged, he ordered them to stand and fight. At the approach of British grenadiers, notes his biographer Ron Chernow, the Americans "ran in confusion, dumping muskets, powder horns, tents, and knapsacks without firing a shot." Washington used his riding crop to whip some of his fleeing officers, who refused to heed him.

Finally he was stranded alone on the battlefield with his aides, his troops having fled in fright. Most astonishingly, Washington on horseback stared frozen as fifty British soldiers started to dash toward him from eighty yards away. Seeing his strangely catatonic state, his aides rode up beside him, grabbed the reins of his horse, and hustled him out of danger. In this bizarre conduct, Nathanael Greene saw a suicidal impulse, contending that Washington was "so vexed at the infamous conduct of his troops that he sought death rather than life."

The mind reels at the prospect of him succeeding: what a different history we might have. Chernow concludes, "It was a moment unlike any other in Washington's career, a fleeting emotional breakdown amid battle," which shook him to the core. To Lund, he wrote, "In confidence I tell you that I never was in such an unhappy, divided state since I was born"—and then he explained where he wanted the chimney to be placed in a new room under construction at Mount Vernon.

What to make of the fact that the father of our country once fell prey to suicidal despair? It is a useful reminder that for all of America's natural bounty and good fortune its fate was uncertain at its origin—and it remains so, for democracy is a fragile construct that can be undone. Its survival is not guaranteed. If Washington's deficiencies as a military strategist were balanced by his strength of character, then the episode on the battlefield in Murray Hill must be factored into any consideration of his decisions and conduct, not only of the war but of his presidency. His much-praised humility, which induced him to leave office after two terms, ensuring a peaceful transition of power, may reflect self-knowledge of the darkness in his soul.

Perhaps Washington's postwar efforts to restore his lands helped to heal his soul and contributed to his belated (albeit partial) recognition of the iniquity of slavery. His letters and diaries reveal that in addition to addressing private matters (teeth, money), reflecting on the state of the republic, and keeping records of the trees he tagged on woodland excursions for transplanting to Mount Vernon, he was avid for information about the latest agricultural developments. Convinced that he and other Virginia planters had exhausted the soil by rotating cash crops like tobacco, corn, and wheat, he sought out new scientific methods, in the best Enlightenment tradition. In 1786, he hired an English farmer to teach his laborers "to Plow, Sow; Mow; Reap; Thatch; Ditch; Hedge

&ca in the best manner." But the Englishman, who in his employer's words made "no allowances for the ravages of a nine year's war from which we are but just beginning to emerge," railed against the utility of slave labor, echoing Washington's growing dismay over the peculiar institution. To Robert Morris, a financier and founding father, he wrote, "There is not a man living who wishes more sincerely than I do, to see a plan adopted for the abolition of [slavery]—but there is only one proper and effectual mode by which it can be accomplished, & that is by Legislative authority, and this, as far as my suffrage will go, shall never be wanting." But he did not act on this noble sentiment (and his slaves were not freed until after his death), partly because he wanted to maintain his lavish lifestyle despite a chronic shortage of cash, partly because at the birth of the republic he feared advancing a proposal that might tear it apart—which, of course, slavery was destined to do.

The failings of the founders, two-thirds of whom owned slaves, on this question complicate the genial image of gentlemen-farmers enshrined in American cultural memory. Thomas Jefferson is alternately praised for his political acumen and breadth of learning, spanning architecture, philosophy, horticulture (he sent dogwood seeds to a correspondent in Paris), and much more, and censured

for fathering six children with his slave Sally Hemings—
the only slaves of his who were freed after his death. The
comprehensive knowledge on display in his writings is
integral to the art of diplomacy—a generalist's profession,
prudent statesmanship depending upon familiarity with
a range of fields of inquiry—and Jefferson was certainly
a brilliant diplomat. But it also demands from its practi-
tioners a moral compass, which for the southern founders
was sorely lacking when it came to the issue of slavery.

"Justice will take us millions of intricate moves," the
poet William Stafford wrote, which suggests that one
wrong move, even one made with the best intentions, can
destroy the whole—a notion I keep in my mind on my regular work-related visits to the capital. Sometimes in the
morning, when I run along the National Mall, duplicating
part of our mad dash made long ago to the Washington
Monument, I stop at the Vietnam War Memorial to trace
my finger over the name of Robert Bruce Tufts, my baseball coach's nephew, killed in action on June 14, 1969—the
year before I was confirmed into the Episcopal Church.
One wrong move can be enough to cause a tragedy. Stafford also wrote, "Planting trees is *hedging* with time: you
want it to pass so the trees will be big." No wonder Washington loved dogwoods.

Book Wings

One autumn on a cultural diplomacy mission to Russia, I had occasion to tour Leo Tolstoy's country estate, Yasnaya Polyana, near the town of Tula, a three-hour drive south from Moscow. It was a chilly, sunny morning, and under the yellowing leaves of the birches lining the road to the manor house an amiable guide told me that in 1903 the American politician William Jennings Bryan postponed an audience with the czar to extend his visit here. These towering figures of art and politics discussed nonviolence, Tolstoy declaring that nothing justified the use of force, not even to save the life of a child. War was looming with Japan; another pogrom was under way, this time in Moldova; and Bryan concluded that the secret to Tolstoy's global influence was love, his "shield and sword." Here was the study in which he wrote *War and Peace*, here the ceiling hook from which he planned to hang himself before he converted to Christianity, and here the calendar opened to October 28, 1910, the day on which the aging writer, sick with fever, fled his marriage and estate, resolving to change his life, only to die of pneumonia at the railway station in Astapovo. My guide's colleagues were preparing to celebrate the centenary of his death—a century marked by more bloodshed than any other in history. Pacifism blinded Tolstoy to the need to protect civilians, children in particular, and if idealism in one form or another animated the most complex characters peopling his novels (Konstantin Levin, Count Pierre Bezukhov), it also led him astray in his private life. Where are my blind spots? I wondered, walking toward a clearing he called "the place of the green wand," where he is buried. There are limits to what can be achieved in the name of love.

Cultural diplomacy falls under the rubric of public diplomacy, which the political theorist Joseph Nye defines as "soft power" (in contrast to the exercise of hard—military and economic—power) and which, after 9/11, generated considerable debate in foreign policy circles. The models of soft power developed by the IWP, offering the pedagogy of creative writing as an alternative to the dictates of violent extremist ideologies, landed me on the front lines of what some described as a war of ideas, a clash of civilizations. I did not view this clash as a war, at least not yet (though war is one way for nations to resolve competing claims and ideas), but a dialogue, with far-reaching cultural, geopolitical, and spiritual implications.

Dialogue depends upon listening, and listening is essential not only to cultural exchange, which ideally courses in both directions, but to any creative enterprise. A poem, for example, may begin with the poet hearing something—a word, a phrase, a rhythm—that starts a journey into the unknown. Hence the connection between poets and diplomats: they share a penchant for listening (to the intricacies of language, to the views of others) and then representing, on the page or in person, some vision of their relationship to the whole—to literature, to their country. I am drawn to the tradition of poet-diplomats, which includes the Nobel laureates Saint-John Perse, George Seferis, Pablo Neruda, Czeslaw Milosz, and Octavio Paz; if it is difficult to gauge the influence of their diplomatic work on their poetry, it is reasonable to assume that the knowledge they acquired of the inner workings of government, foreign and domestic, deepened their understanding of the human condition—and the world. In his Nobel lecture, Perse said that "in spite of himself, the poet also is tied to historical events" and "nothing in the drama of his times is alien to him." Perse described his early masterpiece *Anabasis* as "the poem of solitude in action": an apt description of the divided loyalties I feel on my sojourns abroad, between my poetic calling and my responsibilities as director of the IWP. My night and day jobs, if you will. The tension between action and reflection is a familiar literary theme, and if it informs my life it also shapes the IWP's mission, which is to establish fertile conditions for creative work and the exchange of ideas. Between the search for truth integral to literature and the common ground essential to diplomacy, between art and politics, lies terrain yet to be charted by literary critics.

Take *Book Wings*, a project to connect American and Russian writers, directors, and actors, in a performance livestreamed to a global audience. It was conceived by the U.S.-Russia Bilateral Presidential Commission, which Presidents Medvedev and Obama signed into being in 2009, to reset relations between Russia and America. Pledging to move beyond "Cold War mentalities," the Russian Ministry of Foreign Affairs and the State Department established working groups for different sectors, including energy, arms control, counterterrorism, drug trafficking, economic relations, agriculture, the environment, the military, space, and health. I served on the working group for education, sports, mass media, and cultural exchanges, and during introductions at our first meeting in Moscow, in December 2010, in a crowded conference room at the Ministry of Foreign Affairs, a short, wiry, grey-haired man rose to his feet to challenge us. He was Anatoly Smeliansky, director of the renowned Moscow Art Theatre School.

"Over the last twenty years," he said, pacing back and forth, "we've trained a thousand American students in the Stanislavski method, and now I can talk to my daughter every night in Cambridge on Skype. Can't we find some way to meet in the virtual world?"

I seized on his idea, breaking protocol to answer him directly.

"Yes, yes," I said, and for some minutes Anatoly and I traded ideas about what we might create together over the Internet—plays, master classes, seminars. Presently the Russian ambassador and the American undersecretary for public affairs left with their entourages, and the mood lightened in the room. Then the American chief of staff returned to tap me on the shoulder. The undersecretary wished to have a word—not to castigate me for overstepping my bounds, as I feared, but to explore the possibility of forging virtual connections with our Russian counterparts, university to university, theater to theater, writer to writer.

"You make this work," she ordered.

So began an unusual collaboration. Over the next year, via e-mail, Skype, and meetings in Washington and Moscow, Anatoly and I designed an experiment for a virtual environment. He suggested that we invite poets, dramatists, and fiction writers from both countries to create works for the stage on a common theme. With State Department funding, the IWP and the Moscow Art Theatre School invented *Book Wings*, a three-year project to foster a cross-cultural conversation, spark dramatic ideas, and produce works addressing different sides of our shared history. For the first year we commissioned American and Russian poets to write a short play, a poetic sequence, a monologue, a dialogue, or some combination thereof, on the theme of contact, which has both positive and negative connotations: the rush of feeling that comes from constant contact, the loss of personal space, the strangeness of being known and unknown at the same time, and more. Then the poets were provided with literal translations of their counterparts' work, which they polished into scripts for actors and directors from the University of Iowa and the Moscow Art Theatre School to perform in their respective black-box theaters.

Meanwhile technical teams in both cities built a

virtual stage for a live performance so that audiences in Iowa City, in Moscow, and around the world could watch the drama unfold in real time—a confluence of literature, theater, and information technology, available to anyone with access to the Internet, that might help to bridge the gap between two peoples who for more than four decades had regarded each other as mortal enemies.

The show went off without a hitch in March 2012, days after Vladimir Putin's controversial election to a third presidential term, in what international observers regarded as a flawed voting process—marking the beginning of the end of the reset. The breakfast crowd in Iowa City could see a Moscow audience dressed for dinner. The opening Russian skit—a spoof on the hitherto unknown connections between Iowa and Russia, derived from an inventive reading of a *Wikipedia* entry on the makeup of Iowa's population—set a buoyant tone for the performance, which moved seamlessly from stage to stage, world to world, concluding with Anatoly wishing us a pleasant day. He and his friends would march the next morning in protest of Putin's reelection, but for now all was magic.

Book Wings continued against the backdrop of Putin's efforts to restore Russia's status as a great power, diminish American influence, and reconfigure the international order. Tensions rose between Moscow and Washington over one issue after another, and though it was a commonplace to bemoan the failure of the reset, the State Department nevertheless encouraged me to keep seeking connections with Russian writers and educational institutions. In preparation for a mission in April 2014, during the diplomatic crisis precipitated by Russia's annexation of Crimea, I read Tolstoy's *Sevastopol Sketches*, three stories inspired by his service during the yearlong siege of the Crimean city (1854–1855). Military life proved to be a costly adventure for the writer, his gambling losses forcing him to sell the mansion at Yasnaya Polyana to a local landowner, who dismantled, transported, and rebuilt it on his estate. (Tolstoy proceeded to gamble away some of the proceeds from the sale.) It also provided him with material. *Sevastopol Sketches*, which earned him acclaim as the first modern war correspondent, is a kind of sketch for *War and Peace*, a preparatory study without which his epic masterpiece might never have taken shape. In the opening story he uses an intimate form of address, the second-person narrative, to reveal the true horror of war, capturing its sights, sounds, smells, and textures. About his visit to a hospital, for example, he writes:

The doctors are engaged on the horrible but beneficent work of amputation. You will see the sharp, curved knife enter the healthy white flesh; you will see the wounded man come back to life with terrible heartrending screams and curses. You will see a doctor's assistant toss the amputated arm into a corner, and you will see, in the same room, another wounded man on a stretcher, watching the operation, and writhing and groaning, not so much with physical pain, as with the mental torture of anticipation. You will see ghastly sights that will rend your soul; you will see war, not with its orderly, beautiful, and brilliant ranks, its music and beating drums, its waving banners, its generals on prancing horses, but war in its real aspect of blood, suffering, and death. . . .

Scenes like this fed his growing belief in the futility of war, and his concern for the low morale of the Russian troops. The allied forces of Britain, France, and the Ottoman Empire suffered grave losses while besieging Sevastopol, the final battle in their defeat of Russia (a defeat repeated nearly a century later when Nazi Germany overran the city), and yet Tolstoy discerned in the allied prisoners he met a sense of purpose lacking in his countrymen, notwithstanding their fighting spirit. His biographer Rosamund Bartlett observes that he became "convinced . . . that Russia either needed fundamental reform, or would collapse." This required a spiritual transformation, the founding of a new religion, the outlines of which he described in his diary:

> Yesterday a conversation about divinity and faith led me to a great and stupendous idea, the realisation of which I feel capable of devoting my whole life to. This idea is the foundation of a new religion corresponding to the development of mankind—the religion of Christ, but purged of dogma and mystery, a practical religion, not promising future bliss but providing bliss on earth. I realise that to bring this idea to fruition will take generations of people working consciously towards this goal. One generation will bequeath this idea to the next, and one day fanaticism or reason will implement it. Working consciously to unite people with religion is the foundation of the idea which I hope will occupy me.

Bartlett suggests that "all of Tolstoy's future career is here," and it strikes me that his project was close in spirit to *The Life and Morals of Jesus of Nazareth*, Thomas Jefferson's edited version of the New Testament, a cut-and-paste job highlighting the Savior's humanity at the expense of his

miracle stories. In my travels I heard, repeatedly, that at decisive moments in American and Russian history there have
been points of convergence. Tolstoy's musings on faith, for
example, date from the same time period in which Whitman published his first edition of "Song of Myself," propos-
ing among other things the establishment of a new form
of civic religion; within a few years, Whitman had forged a
new style of war reportage, collected in *Memoranda During the War*, that bears a strong resemblance to Tolstoy's
war writings. Indeed *Sevastopol Sketches* and *Memoranda
During the War* conclude in a similar fashion, with single
sentences of several hundred words apiece detailing the le-
thal consequences of war. Tolstoy notes that when the Russian forces were ordered to abandon the city to the invading
army, "the instinct to get away from this dreadful place of
death as quickly as possible was present in the soul of each,"
and then he catalogues the men in whom this sentiment
was present: a soldier dying among the wounded, a militia-
man clearing a path for a general, a sailor squeezed in a
crowd, an officer on a stretcher, an artilleryman pushing
his gun down a bank into the roadstead, sailors who have
just scuttled their ships. And Whitman summons the million dead from fields and woods and valleys, from terraces
and ravines and bridges, from battlefields and graves and

rivers—"the dead, the dead, the dead—*our* dead." All were sacrificed in a war that led to further conjunctions: Czar Alexander, who freed the serfs two years before Lincoln issued the Emancipation Proclamation, wrote several letters to the president pledging his support, insisting that the fate of the world depended upon the preservation of the Union.

The legacy of the Civil War endures in America—in racial tensions; in the political division between North and South; in debates over affirmative action, racial profiling, race-based inequities in the judicial system—just as the fallout from Russia's defeat in the Crimean War continues to shape its body politic. Putin would not have dared to annex Crimea if he did not think his people would support him—and they did, thanks in part to the Kremlin's propaganda. My Russian friends were appalled by their media's portrayal of Western perfidy—how America, the European Union, and NATO had conspired to humiliate Russia in the chaotic aftermath of the Cold War—which buttressed Putin's claim to be rectifying wrongs committed against the former superpower. To explain Putin's high approval ratings, one writer told me her hairdresser was so proud of the annexation of Crimea that her breasts had swelled two sizes!

Such patriotism informed the work of Pavel Svinyin

(1787–1839), an artist and writer who, as a young man attached to the Russian Consulate in Philadelphia from 1811 to 1813, produced a book of impressions and watercolors, *A Russian Paints America*. Friend to Pushkin and Gogol, Svinyin chronicled the New World at a key moment in history, his tour coinciding with the War of 1812—though he wrote more about the American political system, religion, slavery, and steamboats than war. The editors of *A Russian Paints America* note that Svinyin "was unable to find the Russian equivalents for the American tree varieties and was forced to use a transliteration of English names. He writes of the *dog vud* tree. In modern Russian 'dogwood' (*Cornus gen.*) is translated *kizil*. It is not surprising that he was unaware of the name, as dogwood trees can be found in Russia only in Crimea and the Caucasus"—two places that for security reasons the U.S. Embassy would not allow me to visit.

But if I had gone to Sevastopol? A Russian woman working in the cultural affairs office of the embassy, who had escorted me to schools and universities in Moscow, promised to photograph a *kizil* on a weekend jaunt to the seaside resort. Alas, she did not find one.

Seven Star Mountain

Seven Star Mountain, a dormant volcano occupying seven peaks in Taiwan, is covered with silver grass (*Miscanthus sinensis*), a legacy of fires set in the Qing dynasty (1644–1912) to discourage thieves from mining its sulfur deposits—a critical ingredient in the manufacturing of gunpowder. The volcano lies in Yangmingshan National Park, which takes up 115 square kilometers in Taipei, and on a cool, sunny morning in February 2015, just before the Lunar New Year, a retired spy was waiting in the visitor-center parking lot to guide me and a young woman from the Ministry of Culture to the only Asian dogwood (*Cornus kousa*) growing in the park. Lieutenant Colonel Liu Teng-shiang, a small, white-haired man who had devoted his career in military intelligence to finding spies from the mainland, had already made one round trip, at daybreak, to clear a path to the tree. We followed him along the ridge, past a shrine to fallen soldiers and a bunker from the Japanese occupation, then down a trail that kept crossing an S-shaped dirt road, which had been used by Japanese artillery in World War II.

Colonel Liu claimed to have walked over every meter of the park, once known as Grass Mountain and renamed in 1950 after a Ming dynasty philosopher. He had surveyed its mountains and valleys, waterfalls and lakes, gathering information about its flora and fauna—hundreds of species of ferns, birds, and butterflies, along with bamboo vipers and cobras. He laughed off the official's complaint about our brisk pace down the trail, which dated from ancient times, when men carried twenty kilos of fish apiece from the sea to Taipei—a seven-hour hike, he said in admiration. Puffs of steam and the odor of sulfur rose from fumaroles and hot springs. The Japanese, he said, were reputed to have buried vast quantities of stolen gold by the trail, among the wild peonies and dragon vines. *But my enemy is Chinese*, he added, pointing at a mountain, where the air force monitored thousands of missiles aimed from the mainland toward Taiwan.

This was my first visit to the Republic of China, after numerous journeys to the People's Republic of China (PRC), and I felt much freer in the successor state to the Qing dynasty than I did on the mainland. The array of

English titles for sale in a multistory bookstore in Taipei, for example, was a welcome change from what was on offer in Beijing, and I cherished having access to Western news sites blocked in the PRC. Alice, the perky official from the Ministry of Culture who escorted me around the island, dispensed information with an alacrity impossible to imagine across the Taiwan Strait, a flash point between Beijing and Washington.

I was coming from another hot spot, Karachi, where Indian and Pakistani writers from the IWP had appeared onstage together at a literature festival, their ease and banter with one another a counter to the extremists in both countries who were determined to sow discord between Hindus and Muslims. What endured in my memory, though, was a conversation at a buffet dinner on the first night of the festival, in the garden of a swank hotel overlooking a lagoon fringed with mangroves. I was seated between two German nuns who ran an orphanage in a Taliban-haunted district of the city, and as they discussed the difficulties of raising and educating children who were otherwise condemned to lead miserable lives, I felt the ground shift underfoot. Daily they faced the danger of abduction, rape, or murder, and yet these faithful women betrayed no outward sign of fear. Their ministry in an Islamic country, in the name of Christ Jesus, was a foil to the hard men who would impose on others an aberrant vision of their faith. Of all the courageous individuals I had met in war zones, none impressed me more than the pair of demure women who kept insisting that I try different Pakistani dishes.

In Yangmingshan it was difficult to distinguish between the ribbons of mist laid across the mountain, courtesy of nearly two hundred days of rain a year, and the steam rising from fumaroles, the smell of which brought back a day from twenty years before, when Lisa and I had walked over a lava flow at the southern tip of the Big Island of Hawai'i. She was pregnant with Hannah, and as mist formed around us from the red-hot earth beneath our feet I hoped that this conjunction of new life and the creation of new land augured well for our daughter.

The same could not be said of the PRC's island-manufacturing scheme in the South China Sea, its overlapping claims with Brunei, Malaysia, the Philippines, Taiwan, and Vietnam being the source of escalating tensions in the Pacific. China's claim to these rich fishing waters, under which lay vast, if largely unexplored, oil and natural gas reserves, rested on an inventive interpretation of international law, which extended the twelve-mile limit on territorial waters nearly a hundredfold through the creation of seven artificial islands in the sparsely inhabited Spratly archipelago—an ambitious dredging operation to transform coral reefs and rock formations with names like Fiery Cross and Mischief Reef into islands with airstrips, lighthouses, and radar. The U.S. Navy, which guarantees the security of five trillion dollars in annual trade passing through these sea-lanes, was preparing to test China's willingness to defend its "great wall of sand." Beijing dismissed Washington's warnings against militarizing its claims in the South China Sea and went on building up its naval fleet, adding new classes of destroyers, cruisers, submarines, and an aircraft carrier, inspiring its neighbors to take countermeasures. The Philippines brought a case against China in the Permanent Court of Arbitration in The Hague (which would eventually rule in favor of the Philippines); Japan passed security legislation effectively ending its official policy of pacifism; and, ironically, Vietnam secured American funding to buy U.S. patrol boats. Of particular concern to Colonel Liu, however, was the crisis in the East China Sea, not far beyond the mist-beribboned mountain in our sights. If tensions over the Senkaku/Diayo/Diaoyutai islands, a group of rocks and uninhabited islands claimed by China, Japan, and Taiwan, led to war between China and Japan, Taiwan would be the loser. What a precarious place to live.

We walked to a lava plateau, where a sign in Chinese and English explained that nature had sculpted the ridge above us into the form of a traditional Chinese lion stretched out on its belly, gazing at a gigantic ball in the distance. All I could see was steam rising from fumaroles. On we marched for close to an hour, stopping in a valley at the edge of a marsh. Colonel Liu instructed me to take off my shoes to wade through the water to the dogwood, which I did not recognize until he pointed to its four trunks. These he likened to the four directions of the wind. I was not so sure. Indeed I was disappointed by its very ordinariness: to hike this far to run my fingers over the bark of a leafless tree seemed quixotic. The colonel, though, seemed ecstatic. He suspected that a bird passing over had seeded the dogwood, marveling at the fact that it was the only one in the park. And his enthusiasm colored my view for the rest of the hike, over stone bridges, past waterfalls, and along a cement waterway. I was thinking of the dogwood as a metaphor for the fragility of life, when the colonel presented me with a gift: a laminated series of photographs he had taken of the dogwood in winter and spring, with close-ups of its flowers and fruit. Then he began to sing, in English: *Thank you for the sun. Thank you for the tree. Thank you for the mountains. Thank you for me.* He had a pleasant voice, and on the third time through he encouraged me to join in. On the eve of the Year of the Sheep I was filled with gratitude.

Earthquake

My bed was shaking, and when I got to my feet the floor kept moving. I stood in the dark, swaying, momentarily unable to remember if I was in Pakistan or Taiwan. Then it came to me: the coastal city of Hualien, the last stop on my tour of the island nation. The epicenter of the earthquake, measuring 6.2 on the Richter scale, was just offshore, and so my room in the Just Sleep Hotel kept swaying for fifteen seconds, after which I could not get back to sleep. I lay in bed thinking about our excursion the day before through the Tunnel of Nine Turns, above Taroko Gorge, a magnificent natural formation carved from marble. Over a quarter of Taiwan's hundred tallest peaks lie within the boundaries of Taroko National Park, according to the guide hired by the Ministry of Culture. She explained that the park owed its origins to the Chinese Civil War, which did not end when Chang Kai-shek evacuated his government and two million followers to Taiwan in 1949.

Fearing an attack by Mao's army, Chang ordered a road to be built through the mountains; more than two hundred soldiers died during its construction. The narrow road through the gorge was slick with water dripping from cracks in the walls and crowded with tourists from the mainland—white-helmeted men and women carrying on a tradition of overrunning the island once known as Formosa, said the guide with a tight smile, that dated from the seventeenth century, when the Han Chinese began to settle it. Emerging from the tunnel, I walked to the cliff to peer down at the river. Marble gleamed on both sides of the greenish water, and swallows flew from their nests in the canyon. Our guide, a young woman who had quit her job selling marble in a local factory, believing the work to be too dangerous, was volunteering in the park until she found another job. But she had been doing this for two years, and it seemed that she had given up hope of anything changing in her life. She was living with her parents; she said she had no interest in raising a family; she could not imagine moving to another city. What jolts us awake? This was what I reflected on in the dark.

Still sleepless at first light, I went for a run, heading toward the Pine Garden, where Japanese kamikaze pilots occupying Taiwan during World War II would get drunk the night before their final missions. But before I reached the site of infamy I turned right at a bridge and ran along the river to the Pacific, where a freighter was being unloaded and men were fishing from a jetty. At the sight of the calm surface of the sea my thoughts turned to the Fukushima nuclear disaster: in March 2011, a tsunami trigged by a 9.0 earthquake off the coast of Japan struck the power plant, causing core meltdowns in three of its six reactors—the worst nuclear event since the Chernobyl meltdown in 1986. A significant amount of radioactive material was released, contaminating the air and water; three hundred thousand people were evacuated from the area; the cleanup might take decades, experts warned, costing tens of billions of dollars; a memorial garden of dogwoods transplanted from America would commemorate the victims of the tragedy.

A bell rang three times as I walked out on the jetty. An old man with a fishing rod was following his son and granddaughter over the rocks, and he was but a step away from the water's edge when he slipped and fell, nearly splitting open his forehead. His son pulled him to his feet and dusted him off.

There was something about the scene that called to mind an experience from the summer of my high school graduation. My family had left for North Carolina, and on the day the movers came to load our furniture onto a truck I joined a friend at Buttermilk Falls to smoke some Afghan hash. *Dappled* was the word I used to describe the sunlight filtering through the trees lining India Brook, inspiring a giggling fit from my stoned friend. The hash he had scored was quite strong, and after we smoked another bowl I went to sit on a ledge under a waterfall as if in a shower, gazing through cascading sheets of water at the sky and trees. I was perfectly content. And I was still high when I returned to our empty house that night. The light bulb hanging from the ceiling in the living room cast weird shadows on the wooden floor, which creaked as I paced back and forth, a welter of emotions rising in me. Severing another tie to childhood mitigated my excitement at the prospect of leaving for college, perhaps because I was falling in love with a girl from Bedminster. How will this work? I wondered endlessly, suspecting— rightly, as it turned out—that we were not meant for each other. For some reason the movers had left behind the grandfather clock, which was ticking loudly in the corner, and all at once I felt a presence in the room that made the hair on the back of my neck stand up. The bare walls seemed to swell; there was a humming in the air; I feared for my sanity.

"Is someone here?" I whispered. Nothing. The clock ticked. I bolted out the door and stood in the garden, contemplating the black outline of the saltbox against the sky until my friend drove up. Off we went to smoke another bowl, in honor of the end of something.

In the morning, though, waking on his sofa, I was surprised to discover in myself a longing to duplicate the sense of awe I had felt the night before, to court whatever divinity had revealed itself to me in the living room. But when I returned to our house the new owners would not let me in—they were busy preparing for the arrival of their furniture—and so I wandered in the back field among the rows of black walnut seedlings my father and I had planted the spring before. It took hours to mow five acres of grass on a tractor, and every week I weaved recklessly around the seedlings, nicking and killing at least a third of them, bouncing up and down. "You'll end up with truck driver's kidneys," my father warned—to no avail. Now to my chagrin I could not muster any feelings beyond discomfort in the heat of the sun and numbness in the depths of my soul. I spent the rest of the day getting high with my friend.

Forty years later, I walked to the end of the jetty and stood by the sea, marveling at its flat grey surface. A local wit dubbed this earthquake the Valentine's Day limited edition; a much larger one lay in the offing. I gazed eastward, longing for home.

Heart Condition

A pair of kousa dogwoods frames the entrance to City Park Pool in Iowa City. I had not noticed them before the summer evening when my younger daughter, Abby, and I went there for a swim. The trees were in blossom, swirls of white chalices atop four trunks apiece, kin to the dogwood I had seen on Seven Star Mountain. The sight offered relief from my anxiety over Abby's deteriorating health. In the last year she had fallen prey to various ailments (fatigue, dizziness, brain fog, upset stomach, low pulse rate and blood pressure), growing so weak that she could barely get out of bed in the morning. We spent a fortune taking her to different doctors, none of whom could diagnose her condition. Indeed her pediatrician dismissed her complaints as those of any fourteen-year-old, which made her feel worse. On a summer evening, though, in the presence of dogwood blossoms, I felt at peace, and this reinforced the delight I took in watching her jump from the high dive into the water. But when I saw how skinny she had become—her arms and legs were thin as twigs, her ribs protruded—I shuddered in fear.

It was in some respects a miracle that Abby was even here. Hers was a complicated birth, a perfect knot having formed in the umbilical cord, which was wrapped around her neck when she emerged, silent. Neither Lisa nor I suspected that anything was amiss until the midwife let us see our baby for just a moment—she was not breathing—before whisking her out of the room.

"What's the matter with her?" Lisa cried.

I followed the midwife into the corridor, where a neonatal team was waiting, and there I watched a doctor shout at Abby, lifting her in the air to slap her bottom. Seconds passed, which seemed to extend into eternity, and then she gasped. A nurse placed an oxygen mask over her face, and she was wheeled on a gurney to the intensive care unit, where she would remain for the better part of a week, until her lungs began to work on their own. A medical resident, checking on Lisa, blithely said that our daughter was the victim of bad luck; in the next twenty-four hours she would have to declare herself for life, or else . . . Lisa burst into tears. The resident left the room, oblivious, it seemed, to the effect of her words.

Unhelpful commentary from the medical profession—we would grow accustomed to this when Abby, a gifted singer, dancer, and actress who had worked in professional theater from the age of ten, could not finish an intensive summer program with the Houston Ballet. Myriad tests produced inconclusive results, so her pediatrician referred her to a psychiatrist, who sent her back to the pediatrician, who referred her in turn to an endocrinologist, a gastroenterologist, and a nutritionist, none of whom could figure out what was wrong. Abby underwent a colonoscopy and an endoscopy, tried gluten- and lactose-free diets, changed medications and dosages for her thyroid disease. Nothing helped. Job's Old Testament cry to his friends became my refrain—"You are worthless physicians, all of you." Lisa stayed up late to scour the Web for information, Abby struggled to stay cheerful, and I seized on any sign of improvement in her demeanor to imagine that her recovery was near at hand. Meantime there were trips to the emergency room, phone calls to specialists, and consultations with therapists, homeopaths, and an acupuncturist; a functional doctor ordered tests costing thousands of dollars, which insurance did not cover. Our despair mounted, as well as our bills, and still an accurate diagnosis remained elusive.

"'Hope' is the thing with feathers - / That perches in the soul," Emily Dickinson wrote—lines I chanted morning and night, along with prayers that my daughters would enjoy long, healthy, and productive lives. I was becoming an expert in the field of hope (which, as the saying goes, is not a strategy), monitoring Abby's condition for anything to grasp on to. "For there is hope for a tree," Job said, "if it is cut down, that it will sprout again, and that its shoots will not cease." In my imagination the blooming dogwoods at the pool acquired talismanic significance.

Lisa had tried to make an appointment for Abby at the Mayo Clinic, which was booked until October. Miraculously, it seemed, less than a week after our evening swim, we learned of an opening because of a last-minute cancellation. Lisa immediately drove Abby to Rochester, Minnesota, where she was given a preliminary diagnosis of postural orthostatic tachycardia syndrome (POTS)—a puzzling dysfunction of the autonomic nervous system, first identified as "soldier's heart" during the Civil War. No one in my acquaintance had ever heard of POTS, which afflicts up to three million Americans. (By way of contrast, five million Americans have Alzheimer's disease.) This may explain why the average time to diagnosis is six years, by which point most sufferers have lost all hope. There is an easy test for it: an electrocardiogram is performed on a patient lying on a table, which is then tilted upright; if the patient's heart rate rises by more than fifty beats per minute, the diagnosis is confirmed. Why, we wondered during the lengthy pain-rehabilitation program that Abby underwent with other teenagers, did the doctors at the teaching hospital in Iowa City never think to test her for POTS?

The treatment for this debilitating condition is unusual: the afflicted are instructed to drink several liters of water a day, increase their intake of salt, exercise, and never discuss how they are feeling. The idea is to create new neural pathways in order to trick the body's nervous system into functioning properly again: to write a new narrative, if you will—which is what occurs after any meaningful experience of art and war, of love and loss. Abby and her new circle of friends, some of them in wheelchairs and hooked up to feeding tubes, thus carried saltshakers to therapy sessions designed to teach them how to manage their symptoms, while we and other parents learned not to ask them how they felt. It seemed to work.

I was visiting Mayo one weekend in August when news broke that the Islamic State, having conquered large swathes of land in Iraq and Syria and incurred the wrath of the civilized world with its videotaped beheadings of Western journalists, had encircled tens of thousands of fleeing Yazidis on Mount Sinjar, in northern Iraq. The Yazidis, a tiny religious minority incorporating elements of Zoroastrianism, Christianity, and Islam, believe that after the biblical flood Noah's Ark made landfall on Mount Sinjar, and on this sacred place of refuge they waited in searing heat, without food, water, or medicine, for American, British, and Iraqi helicopters to airdrop supplies and Kurdish forces to lead them to safety. Not all escaped: hundreds of women and girls, some the ages of my daughters, were enslaved by the warriors. Anxious as I was about Abby, I realized that in the scheme of things we were comparatively blessed.

On Labor Day weekend, just before City Park Pool closed for the season, Abby and I went for a last swim. She had gained back some weight, and though her recovery would take months, if not years, she was definitely improving. The dogwoods at the entrance were thick with fruit, which would ripen in the next month. I made a mental note to look online for recipes for dogwood-berry sauce and jam, then paid our admission fee and joined my daughter in the pool.

Epilogue

"On the last day of the world," W. S. Merwin wrote, "I would want to plant a tree." Here at the end of my book I pick up a small plastic bag containing a dozen seeds of flowering dogwood, a gift from a friend at the State Department. I will plant them in a row along the fence in our backyard, in the partial shade of the white oaks towering overhead. Flowering dogwoods are not considered winter-hardy in eastern Iowa, but with rising temperatures from the greenhouse effect extending the range of *Cornus florida* I have decided to mulch the bed with sawdust to protect the seeds over the winter, and when the snow melts next spring I will clear the ground for seedlings to emerge. These I will water regularly, under a cloth hung to shield them from the sun; by late summer, they should be strong enough to survive on their own. In the space between the fence and the ravine at the edge of our property I may plant other species of dogwoods better suited to Iowa—grey, silky, pagoda, Tatarian, cornelian cherry, red osier—to bring more color and light to this patch of land above the Iowa River coursing through the city.

The white oaks in our neighborhood are succumbing to wilt, and there is no telling how long the stately pair in my yard will last. The one to the east has already withstood a lightning strike that sheared off a third of its trunk, the falling branches destroying my daughters' play structure and swing set; the one to the north is thick with dead limbs, which must be removed before they break off in a storm and crash into the garage. These dogwoods will thus eventually grow in full sun, producing more flowers in the spring and brighter colors in the fall, attracting birds, squirrels, raccoons, and deer from the ravine. At the first sign of disease, blight or anthracnose or powdery mildew, the dead or dying branches must be pruned and the fallen leaves raked up—which I will do, if I am still around. If not? I will take comfort in the knowledge that something remains.

Selected Bibliography

Ali, Agha Shahid. *The Veiled Suite: The Collected Poems.* New York: W. W. Norton, 2009.

Angelo, Ray. *Botanical Index to the Journal of Henry David Thoreau.* Salt Lake City: Gibbs Smith, 1984.

Barringer, Felicity. "Climate Change Will Disrupt Half of North America's Bird Species, Study Says." *New York Times,* September 9, 2014. A14.

Bartlett, Rosamund. *Tolstoy: A Russian Life.* Boston: Houghton Mifflin Harcourt, 2011.

Bartram Trail Conference. *Bartram Heritage: A Study of the Life of William Bartram by the Bartram Trail Conference, Including the Report to the Heritage, Conservation and Recreation Service, U.S. Department of the Interior.* Montgomery, AL: Bartram Trail Conference, 1979.

Bishop, Elizabeth. *Poems.* Edited by Saskia Hamilton. New York: Farrar, Straus and Giroux, 2011.

Borges, Jorge Luis. *Professor Borges: A Course on English Literature.* Edited by Martín Arias and Martín Hadis. New York: New Directions, 2013.

Brautigan, Richard. *A Confederate General from Big Sur,*

Dreaming of Babylon, and The Hawkline Monster. Boston: Houghton Mifflin, 1991.

Breton, André. "Constellations." Translated by Jeanie Puleston Fleming and Christopher Merrill. Santa Fe: *Tyuonyi* 8 (1990): 4–14.

Brodsky, Joseph. *Less Than One: Selected Essays.* New York: Farrar, Straus and Giroux, 1986.

Burke, Gregory. *Black Watch.* London: Faber and Faber, 2007.

Campbell, Kurt, and Robert Kagan. "The Obama Administration's Pivot to Asia: A Conversation with Assistant Secretary Kurt Campbell." Foreign Policy Initiative video, 25:25. From the forum "Maintaining America's Global Responsibilities in an Age of Austerity," December 13, 2011. http://www.foreignpolicyi.org/content/obama-administra tions-pivot-asia.

Cappiello, Paul, and Don Shadow. *Dogwoods: The Genus Cornus.* Portland: Timber Press, 2005.

Carson, Rachel. *Silent Spring.* Boston: Houghton Mifflin, 2002.

Chase, Philander D. "Thoughts of Home: General Washington Kept a Picture of Mount Vernon in His Mind's Eye during the Revolutionary War." *Papers of George Washington,* 1995. http://gwpapers.virginia.edu/history/articles/thoughts-of -home/.

Chernow, Ron. *Washington: A Life.* New York: Penguin Books, 2010.

Cummings, Milton C., Jr. *Cultural Diplomacy and the United States Government: A Survey.* Washington, D.C.: Center for Arts and Culture, 2003.

Darwin, Charles. *The Origin of Species by Means of Natural*

Selection; Or the Preservation of Favoured Races in the Struggle for Life. New York: New American Library, 2003.

De Quincy, Thomas. *Confessions of an English Opium-Eater.* Edited by Barry Milligan. London: Penguin Classics, 2003.

Dickinson, Emily. *The Poems of Emily Dickinson.* Edited by R. W. Franklin. Cambridge, MA: Belknap Press, 1999.

Edwards, Joan, Dwight Whitaker, Sarah Klionsky, and Marta J. Laskowski. "Botany: A Record-Breaking Pollen Catapult." *Nature* 435 (May 12, 2005): 164.

Fowles, John. *Daniel Martin.* New York: Little, Brown, 2010.

Fowles, John, and Frank Horvat. *The Tree.* Boston: Little, Brown, 1979.

Frost, Robert. *The Poetry of Robert Frost: The Collected Poems.* Edited by Edward Connery Lathem. New York: Henry Holt, 2002.

Hallock, Thomas. *From the Fallen Tree: Frontier Narratives, Environmental Politics, and the Roots of a National Pastoral, 1749–1826.* Chapel Hill: University of North Carolina Press, 2003.

Hamer, Richard. *A Choice of Anglo-Saxon Verse.* London: Faber and Faber, 1970.

Hayden, Robert. *Collected Poems.* Edited by Frederick Glaysher. New York: Liveright, 2013.

Hesse, Hermann. *Demien: The Story of Emil Sinclair's Youth.* Translated by Michael Roloff and Michael Lebeck. New York: Harper Perennial Modern Classics, 2009.

———. *Wandering: Notes and Sketches.* Translated by James Wright. New York: Farrar, Straus and Giroux, 1972.

Hinterthuer, Adam. "Humanity Has Exceeded 4 of 9 'Planetary

Boundaries,' According to Researchers." University of Wisconsin–Madison website, January 15, 2015. www.news.wisc.edu/23409.

Hinton, David, trans. *I Ching: The Book of Change*. New York: Farrar, Straus and Giroux, 2015.

Hopper, Martha G., Edward W. Roessler, and Wallace G. West. *The Mendhams*. Brookside, NJ: Mendham Township Committee, 1964.

Jones, David. *In Parenthesis*. New York: New York Review of Books, 2003.

Kricher, John C., and Gordon Morrison. *A Field Guide to Ecology of Eastern Forests*. Boston: Houghton Mifflin, 1988.

Kunitz, Stanley. *A Kind of Order, a Kind of Folly: Essays and Conversations*. Boston: Atlantic Monthly Press, 1975.

———. *Next-to-Last Things: New Poems and Essays*. Boston: Atlantic Monthly Press, 1985.

Kunitz, Stanley, with Genine Lentine. *The Wild Braid: A Poet Reflects on a Century in the Garden*. New York: W. W. Norton, 2005.

Little, Charles E. *The Dying of the Trees: The Pandemic in America's Forests*. New York: Viking Penguin, 1995.

Little, Elbert L. *National Audubon Society Field Guide to North American Trees*. New York: Alfred A. Knopf, 1980.

Márai, Sándor. *Embers*. Translated by Carol Brown Janeway. New York: Alfred A. Knopf, 2001.

Markle, Minor M., III. "The Macedonian Sarissa, Spear, and Related Armor." *American Journal of Archaeology* 81, no. 3 (Summer 1977): 323–339.

Matthews, William. *Foreseeable Futures*. Boston: Houghton Mifflin Company, 1987.

Mayborn, William. "The Pivot to Asia: The Persistent Logics of Geopolitics and the Rise of China." *Journal of Military and Strategic Studies* 15, no. 4 (October 2014): 76–101.

McCullough, David. *1776*. New York: Simon & Schuster, 2005.

Merwin, W. S. "The House and the Garden: The Emergence of a Dream." *Kenyon Review Online* (Fall 2010). www.kenyon review.org/kr-online-issue/2010-fall/selections/the-house -and-garden-the-emergence-of-a-dream/.

———. *Migration: New and Selected Poems*. Port Townsend, WA: Copper Canyon Press, 2007.

———. *The Miner's Pale Children*. New York: Henry Holt, 1994.

Miyagawa, Shigeru, Shiro Ojima, Robert C. Berwick, and Kazuo Okanoya. "The Integration Hypothesis of Human Language Evolution and the Nature of Contemporary Languages." *Frontiers in Psychology* (June 9, 2014). http://journal .frontiersin.org/Journal/10.3389/fpsyg.2014.00564/full.

Moerman, Daniel E. *Native American Ethnobotany*. Portland: Timber Press, 1998.

Morrow Lindbergh, Anne. *Bring Me a Unicorn: Diaries of Anne Morrow Lindbergh, 1922–1928*. New York: Harcourt Brace Jovanovich, 1972.

Oswalt, Christopher M., Jonja N. Oswalt, and Christopher W. Woodall. "An Assessment of Flowering Dogwood (*Cornus florida* L.) Decline in the Eastern United States." *Open Journal of Forestry* 2, no. 2 (2012): 41–53.

Ouchley, Kelby. *Flora and Fauna of the Civil War: An Environmental Guide*. Baton Rouge: Louisiana State University Press, 2010.

Paz, Octavio. *Convergences: Essays on Art and Literature*. Translated by Helen Lane. London: Bloomsbury, 1987.

Perse, St.-John. *Collected Poems.* Translated by W. H. Auden et al. Princeton: Princeton University Press, 1971.

Petrides, George A. *A Field Guide to Trees and Shrubs.* Boston: Houghton Mifflin, 1972.

Pound, Ezra. *Selected Poems of Ezra Pound.* New York: New Directions, 1957.

Ranney, Thomas G., Larry F. Grand, and John L. Knighten. "Susceptibility of Cultivars and Hybrids of Kousa Dogwood to Dogwood Athracnose and Powdery Mildew." *Journal of Arboriculture* 21, no. 1 (January 1995): 11–16.

Reynolds, David S. *Walt Whitman's America: A Cultural Biography.* New York: Alfred A. Knopf, 1995.

Roethke, Theodore. *The Collected Poems of Theodore Roethke.* New York: Anchor Books, 1975.

———. *Straw for the Fire: From the Notebooks of Theodore Roethke, 1943–1963.* Selected and arranged by David Wagoner. Port Townsend, WA: Copper Canyon Press, 2006.

Schell, Jonathan. *The Fate of the Earth.* New York: Alfred A. Knopf, 1982.

Schimmel, Annemarie. *Rumi's World: The Life and Work of the Great Sufi Poet.* Boston: Shambhala Publications, 1992.

Stafford, William. *Sound of the Ax: Aphorisms and Poems by William Stafford.* Edited by Vincent Wixon and Paul Merchant. Pittsburgh: University of Pittsburgh Press, 2014.

Steffen, Will, et al. "Planetary Boundaries: Guiding Human Development on a Changing Planet." *Science* 247, no. 6,223 (January 15, 2015): 1–17. http://science.sciencemag.org /content/347/6223/1259855.

Step, Edward. *Wayside and Woodland Trees: A Pocket Guide to the British Sylva*. London: F. Warne, 1907.

Strand, Mark. *Reasons for Moving, Darker, & The Sargentville Notebook: Poems*. New York: Alfred A. Knopf, 1992.

Thayer, Theodore. *Colonial and Revolutionary Morris County*. Morristown, NJ: Morris County Heritage Commission, 1975.

Thomas, David T. "Horticultural and Other Uses of Dogwoods." Accessed June 21, 2014. http://www4.ncsu.edu/~qyxiang/cornushorticulture.html.

Thoreau, Henry David. *The Journal of Henry David Thoreau*. Edited by Bradford Torrey and Francis H. Allen. Salt Lake City: Gibbs Smith, 1984.

Tolstoy, Leo. *Sevastopol Sketches*. Translated by Louise Maude and Aylmer Maude. New York: Digireads Publishing, 2013.

Tudge, Colin. *The Tree: A Natural History of What Trees Are, How They Live, and Why They Matter*. New York: Crown Publishers, 2006.

Wang Wei. *The Selected Poems of Wang Wei*. Translated by David Hinton. New York: New Directions, 2008.

Whitman, Walt. *Leaves of Grass*. New York: Modern Library, 2001.

———. *Memorandum During the War*. Edited by Peter Coviello. New York: Oxford University Press, 2006.

Wilson, Edward O. *Biophilia: The Human Bond with Other Species*. Cambridge: Harvard University Press, 1984.

Wingfield-Hayes, Rupert. "China's Island Factory." *BBC News*, September 9, 2014. www.bbc.co.uk/news/resources/idt-1446c419-fc55-4a07-9527-a6199f5dc0e2.

Acknowledgments

Thanks first and foremost to my editor, Barbara Ras, who offered to publish my meditations on dogwoods, provided wise counsel during the writing process, and then waited patiently for me to turn in the manuscript, which she read with her customary brilliance. There is no greater pleasure for a writer than to work with an editor who understands what a book might become.

Grace Labatt Parazzoli's superb copyedits spared me many forms of embarrassment. And I was fortunate to have the gifted Sarah Nawrocki shepherd my book through production.

Thanks as well to Jenny Armit, Bishop Chrysostomos, Mary Depew, Lisa DuPree, Ed Folsom, Tom Gavin, Tim Gustafson, Robert Irwin, John Keller, Jim Leach, Addie Leak, Lieutenant Colonel Liu Teng-shiang (ret.), Jay McCulloch, William and Paula Merwin, Mike Munro, Richard Olsen, Lee Oser, Ann Rickets, Jill Staggs, Bill

Wadsworth, Alice Wang, Sun Wei, Rex Weiner, and Jonathan Wilcox, who contributed ideas, information, and logistical support critical to the writing of this book. Any errors of fact or judgment in these pages are mine alone.

Patricia Caswell, Sharyn Lonsdale, Linda Mansperger, and Bruce Rogers hosted me at the Hermitage Artist Retreat on the Gulf Coast of Florida, and I am very grateful to them for the gift of time and space in which this book took shape.

I am also grateful to the editors of the following publications: *Poets & Writers; POROI; Slice; Theatre Design & Technology*; and *Tin House*, in which portions of this book first appeared. "A Route of Evanescence" appeared in somewhat different form in *Mad Heart, Be Brave: On the Work of Agha Shahid Ali*, edited by Kazim Ali (Ann Arbor: University of Michigan Press, 2016). Part of "Besieged" was first published in *Writing Creative Nonfiction*, edited by Philip Gerard (Cincinnati: Story Press, 2001).

CHRISTOPHER MERRILL is the author of six collections of poetry, including *Watch Fire*, for which he received the Lavan Younger Poets Award from the Academy of American Poets; many edited volumes and books of translations; and five previous works of nonfiction, among them *Only the Nails Remain: Scenes from the Balkan Wars*, *Things of the Hidden God: Journey to the Holy Mountain*, and *The Tree of the Doves: Ceremony, Expedition, War*. His work has been translated into nearly forty languages, his journalism appears widely, and his honors include a Chevalier of the Order of Arts and Letters. As director of the International Writing Program at the University of Iowa, Merrill has conducted cultural diplomacy missions to more than fifty countries. He serves on the U.S. National Commission for UNESCO, and in 2012 President Barack Obama appointed him to the National Council on the Humanities.